THE STRUCT
A HANDBOOK OF

THE STRUCTURE OF ENGLISH: A HANDBOOK OF ENGLISH GRAMMAR

by
Michael Newby

CAMBRIDGE
UNIVERSITY PRESS

PUBLISHED BY THE PRESS SYNDICATE OF THE UNIVERSITY OF CAMBRIDGE
The Pitt Building, Trumpington Street, Cambridge CB2 1RP, United Kingdom

CAMBRIDGE UNIVERSITY PRESS
The Edinburgh Building, Cambridge CB2 2RU, United Kingdom
40 West 20th Street, New York, NY 10011-4211, USA
10 Stamford Road, Oakleigh, Melbourne 3166, Australia

First published 1987
Sixth printing 1996

Printed in the United Kingdom by
Athenæum Press Ltd, Gateshead, Tyne & Wear

A catalogue record for this book is available from the British Library

ISBN 0 521 34996 6

The cover photograph is reproduced
courtesy of *Farmers' Weekly*

CE

CONTENTS

To some old best friends (CIL, DJM, NJG)
and to SMN – a best friend above all.

THE STRUCTURE OF ENGLISH

This book is about the way the English language is constructed: its grammar. It tries to describe how, with a limited number of grammatical elements and the rules for putting them together, it is possible for us to make and receive countless millions of different meanings.

As descriptions go, this is the basic version. It is for those who would like to know how the language works but who haven't the time (or don't yet feel ready) for anything more ambitious. There are, of course, some very advanced descriptions indeed. Probably the best-known is *A Grammar of Contemporary English* (Quirk, Greenbaum, Leech & Svartvik: Longman, 1972) – known by those who use it as the 'Quirk Grammar' – and its weightier sequel: *A Comprehensive Grammar of the English Language* (Longman, 1985). These descriptions of how English works are dazzling for the extent of their scholarship and research, awe-inspiring for their insight and precision. They are, for English grammar, what the *Oxford English Dictionary* is for English words: massive reference works, indispensable for the serious student of the language. However, they can be a daunting prospect for the beginner.

There are, nonetheless, many people who would like to know how English is constructed and others who need to know because of the work they do. This book is written for them in the hope that it will help them acquire a useful working knowledge of the subject and, better still, encourage them to examine it more deeply.

It is for the many people who are interested in the English language and who have always meant, one day, to open it up to see how it works. It is for people who may sometimes have been reluctant to risk questions like: 'What *is* a verb?' or 'How, actually, *do* you define a sentence?'. Like many simple questions, the answers can be complex, though this book tries to give the most basic answers possible without losing all sense of the power behind the questions.

The book is, as well, intended for those who have begun a serious study of language and who find they need to know about English grammar from very simple beginnings before they can progress to more complicated works.

It is also for teachers. This is not because many actually teach English grammar any more (at least not in the old way) but rather because of the great interest which has been shown among teachers, especially since the early 1970s, in how children develop and use their language. Surprisingly, children's grammatical development has not received as much attention as other aspects of their language. This is a pity because it helps us understand in a particularly clear and objective way their growth towards adult fluency and literacy. This book may help some interested teachers to look more closely at their pupils' grammar by offering them a set of instruments they can start using straight away.

Although the book is for people just starting to explore grammar, it is written for those who are already expert language-users. We all have language in our heads and, other than looking up meanings and spellings in the dictionary, we rarely need books to tell us how to use it. There is a difference between 'knowing' and 'knowing *about*' and this book tries to reveal part of the language system each of us possesses, inside in our heads and outside in the community of language-sharers. It is not therefore a 'book of rules', since you already know the rules (or how else could you read and comprehend this sentence?), but rather one which tries to help you understand what it is that you know. As it unfolds, you will sometimes be asked to put this knowledge to work. As a user of English you are, after all, an expert witness.

Grammar is not something you can easily see or hear. Rather, it is an organisational power lying underneath the familiar surfaces of our language, hidden from view yet potent in its effects. To help visualise these hidden systems of organisation, the diagrams in the book are based on the analogy of a construction kit. They try to visualise the way the parts from which grammar is made combine together to create language structures. However, mechanical analogies – useful for diagrams – are perhaps less appropriate in explaining grammar than organic ones. Studying grammar is a way of probing beneath the surface of the anatomy of language to see what gives the body life.

And now a warning! Knowing about grammar alone can give only a partial picture of what language is and how it works. People *use* their language for many purposes, so it has a wide variety of different **functions**. This book does not deal in any detail with the relationship between grammar and function. Neither does it look for long at **meaning** – the expression of which is what language is all about. So please don't assume that, having understood what is printed here, you will understand everything there is to know about language. On the other hand, any grasp you may have of the nature of language will be crucially limited without some understanding of its structure.

What's more, a grammar can never be an exact description (perhaps organic analogies are more appropriate than mechanical ones in this). Language is too alive, too mobile, too much used by its speakers and writers for it to be pinned down in books like this. A good grammar will try only to describe clearly the organising systems which control the language found in the community of its users. Furthermore, it will recognise that these systems are not absolute ones. Therefore, no grammar book can be absolutely precise, and people who make them often disagree as to the best ways of describing language structure. One thing this book will not do is enter into theoretical arguments about writing grammars. But you should know that, because it tries to be simple, inevitably it will sometimes describe those structures in ways which, for the expert grammarian, may be open to questions of different interpretation. These questions can be fascinating ones. At this stage, however, they may be more confusing than illuminating.

The book has three sections. *Part One* briefly sets the scene. Without understanding some basic principles about language, and considering a few ideas, it will be harder for you to understand how grammar finds its place as part of our total language system, so if you skip to the next part you may find yourself confused. *Part Two*, the main bulk of the book, tries to describe the structure of the English language, working from its smallest pieces to its biggest ones. *Part Three* is an illustrated glossary. Use this as a reference section so that you can quickly look up a term and see it defined, illustrated and related to the pages where it is first dealt with. In this section, the many technical terms are listed alphabetically, where elsewhere they arrive in a quite different order, one which more systematically explores the ways in which English works. So if you read the glossary alone, you will be missing the best bit of the story.

PART ONE

CHAPTER 1: LABELS

Language is complex, so talking about it can be complicated. In acquiring even a basic understanding of what English is and how it works, you cannot really avoid learning to use some of the many technical terms which are needed to describe its elements and processes. Other people's jargon can be confusing to the outsider, but it actually means something to those who know what they are talking about. It is the same when talking about language.

This 'language-about-language' even has its own technical label: **metalanguage**. *Any* word or phrase used to describe some feature of language is a **metalinguistic** term. Being able to use a metalanguage with confidence means that you can more confidently talk about and understand language itself.

In fact, people already have an extensive metalanguage for everyday use. This is not surprising when you think how important making language is to our daily lives and how often, therefore, we need to talk about it. These metalinguistic terms will be quite familiar:

> **word, sentence, whisper, stammer, article, paragraph, question, response, lisp, comma, conversation, clause, noun, syllable, accent, sermon, shout ...**

Add to this list. Spend a little time writing down all the terms in your own metalanguage. Then keep the list by you as you read through the rest of the book.

As it stands, the list above tells us very little about language. Like opening up a box of parts and simply throwing them into a heap on the table, it has no organisation, being no more than a haphazard collection of words-about-language. However, it becomes more useful in

helping us understand how language works if we put those words into different categories:

word sentence clause noun	whisper shout stammer syllable accent lisp	question response	conversation article sermon	paragraph comma

By sorting the terms like this, we begin to see something of how the systems which organise language structure work. For instance, the second column contains metalinguistic terms which are all to do with the act of speaking; the third starts to list particular language functions; the last, elements of written language; and so on.

Of course, there are many more categories than these in any comprehensive description of language structure. Deciding on what they are, and the metalinguistic terms which belong inside them, is a very important part of constructing a description of the language. We should beware, though, of establishing such categories without asking whether they are really *there*. Do they lie within the language, surprised in hiding by the sudden shaft of light from our torches, or are they *our* labels, imposed by us to make our exploration more convenient? Is there really such a thing as a 'sentence' in the language itself?

Giving something a name, and trying to see the relationship between that and the other names within the description, should help us to know better how the language is made. 'To the mind adrift a new word is a raft.' But names can vary between descriptions; relationships can be explained in different ways. However compelling a description of language might be, we should remember that it *is* only a description and not the intractable, shifting, awkward, living thing itself. Like a photograph, our description may hide as much of the truth as it tries to capture.

This problem has always been close to the heart of the science of language study – which, as you might expect, also has its own label: **linguistics**. This book will not go into the ins and outs of

8

such theory, but it will extend and shape the metalanguage into something more systematic – and so more useful.

The metalanguage used in this book is mainly concerned with items in the first column. However, to see how that part of the whole language system relates to all the rest, we first need to consider some ideas about language in general. In the next chapter we look briefly at such questions as what language is, how people learn to make it and what we mean by *English*. Look out for the metalinguistic terms in it and see how many you already have in your own list.

CHAPTER 2: LANGUAGE INSIDE AND OUT

Making language

Human beings have the capacity to make language. It is given to us, passed on in our genes. Most people use only the language of their native language-community, but we all have it in us to learn other languages too, given the right conditions and incentives to do so.

Language is part of our biological condition. Although used for other things too, it is surprising just how many parts of our bodies are also developed for language. The lungs provide the air which we need to make vocal noise. The complex anatomy in the throat and mouth allows us to modify this vibrating air in order to make the vowels and consonants of speech and to manipulate its melodies, the intonation system. We have ears, of course, to hear what others say as well as to monitor ourselves. We tend to use our hands and arms when we talk and always when we write or type. Our eyes allow us to read and are also important in conversation. Above all, we have a brain and a neurological system of enormous complexity. Together, these allow us both to manipulate our bodies to make language and to process the language code so we can send and receive meaning.

We do not understand all the many forms of communication of creatures other than human beings. What we do know is that nowhere else in the living world can we find a system which works in the same way as does human language. Where other creatures seem to have communication systems which enable them to perform basic functions, only the human species has one which allows such a complexity and range of performance. We know of no other species which can express meanings about past or future events, articulate abstract ideas or construct soap advertisements.

Language on the inside

Language is in our heads. It is *mental behaviour*. Even in our earliest weeks we are attuned to the sounds of speech and have the ability to hear the hubbub of human life, joining in making it ourselves from the outset and gradually coming to learn that it can have coherent meaning and function.

Acquiring and developing this mental behaviour is a very complex process and has given rise to many theories which try to explain how infants learn to become members of the language community. Obviously, *imitation* is important in the developmental process, but that is not the end of the story. Infants and young children also use their powers of *deduction*, working out from what they hear around them the linguistic rules which organise language and testing their new 'theories' as they produce their own expressions and see what kind of reception they get from other people. In fact, our language keeps on developing throughout our lives. (Even in reading this book, you should acquire some new words, a process of vocabulary learning which began when you were between one and two years old.)

Language on the outside

Although it happens in our heads, an individual's language is also the product of the outside world, *social* as much as mental behaviour. From the earliest interactions which take place between the child and its parents, making language is powered by the need to communicate with others. Think of the range of contexts in which children use their language and you have some idea of the variety of influences upon it as it grows to maturity: talking with parents, listening to radio and watching television, arguing with brothers and sisters (older and younger), listening in classrooms, being polite to relatives, playing with kids in the playground, asking teachers questions, reading books ... learning to produce and receive language in these and other situations is part of the socialising process of growing up, helping to connect the individual to the human world.

Our language existed before we were born and will continue after we die. We borrow it. Yet we each use it uniquely, expressing

11

our own individual meanings. We control our language, but we are also controlled by it, since few of us can break free from the way it lets us express what we want to say. Only poets seem able to coax, strain or bully language into abnormal behaviour, revealing its capacity for new meanings, further intricacies, added beauty. For the rest of us, that would merely make us unintelligible and so cut us off from our society.

Languages

The world is full of languages. Some, like English, are major international ones; others, like Welsh, have thousands, not millions, of speakers. Those languages are also written; some are not. Both of those flourish; others decline as their users are absorbed into larger societies and the old ways slip into memory.

A community is partly defined by the language shared by its members. Take that away, and the people lose a crucial part of their identity. Hence the fervour with which minority language groups try to defend their language against outside influence. They are maintaining themselves as a group: their history, their present culture, their future.

It is hard, though, to keep language forever untouched by change, for a language is as mobile as the society which uses it each day. Words grow old and tired as the things they refer to are wheeled off to museums; new ideas clamour for fresh words to label them; ways of putting things, even pronunciation . . . all are in a constant process of evolution. Sometimes, this process is obvious (and all-too-often irritating); usually, however, it is subtle and only half-observed, like a child growing. Listen, for instance, to the way radio announcers used to talk forty years ago. Do they all still talk like that today?

Maybe because of this identification between different peoples and their languages, we sometimes hear claims made for a particular language that it is superior to all others. We like to think that ours is inherently the most 'poetic; expressive; logical; pure; romantic; ancient; complex; precise; beautiful . . .' language in the world, but really there's no evidence to support such assertions. Languages which have been objectively described and studied, be they international languages of great empires or those of tiny communities in far-flung islands lost in distant oceans, all seem to be built on the same design principles, all are equally complex in their systems, and all can be used for the same range of functions in communication, art, science, etc. The pecking order of the world's languages has more to do with history, politics and geography than it has with the languages themselves.

'English'

'English' is the name we give to a tribe of closely-related languages used by millions of people all over the world. Although more people speak Chinese as their mother-tongue, English is used in one form or another by a greater proportion of the world's population than any other of its languages. Some use a form of English as their first language; others use it as a useful second language when they are communicating with someone who does not speak their own. For instance, a French and a Japanese speaker may decide to talk to each other in English as their shared second language.

The tribe has within it many families: national variations of the same common language. Within these families (for example, British and American English) there are still further related groups. Hence the English you speak may be a form of the large family of British Englishes. Or it may be a member of the family of American Englishes, or the ones spoken in Australasia. What your English shares with all the others is known as the **common core**: the great body of sounds and words and structures which, despite their differences, are owned by all the members of the tribe.

No single 'English' is the correct one. In terms of size, American English is the largest family, used as a first language by more people than any other. It could, therefore, be said that American English is now the standard form, though the British may feel a little rebellious in conceding the point. In any case, there are as many different kinds of American English as there are of any other major national family within the tribe.

Dialects

Within a national family of English, people will speak one of its many varieties. If you live in the British Isles, you are likely to speak a variety of English common in a particular region (for example, Scottish, Welsh, Irish, Northern, East Anglian, West Country, etc). These regional varieties are called **dialects**. But even these are very broad categories and within each one we can find a great number of different dialectal variants. Each dialect will be distinguished from all the others by the fact that it contains a number of different words and structural (grammatical) features. There will also tend to be differences in pronunciation between dialects, though this is not necessarily the case (see 'Accents' below).

The differences between all the many dialectal variants within, for example, Scottish English will tend to be less marked than between Scottish English and the range of dialectal variants to be found in the south west of the British Isles. You can see, then, that within the family of British English there are many groups, and within these groups smaller groups. Those who study dialect can distinguish in some cases between the Englishes spoken by people living in different parts of the same town.

Sometimes, a speaker from Belfast may find it a little difficult to understand one from Norwich, and both may occasionally be confused by those from Newcastle or Llanelli. However, since they share the common core, they will be able to communicate. Though speakers from Memphis and Muncie will be conscious of their different ways of using American English, they will never for a moment think of the other as speaking a *foreign* language. French, German, Italian, etc are different language tribes altogether. It should not be forgotten, however, that English itself was a tribe spawned from the inter-marriage between other language tribes a thousand years ago.

Accents

Accents are not the same as dialects, though some would say that accent is a feature of a dialect. Technically, **accent** is the term given to the way a language is pronounced. This page, for example, written in a particular dialect of English, could be read aloud by two people, one American, the other British, and the sound of the language would be different. Furthermore, two British readers of the same page, one from London and the other from Manchester, might also differ in their pronunciation. That said, it is none-theless the case (as you would probably expect) that accents tend to be associated with particular dialects. After all, since dialects are regional varieties of a language, it is unlikely that the people who live in that region will each pronounce their dialect in markedly different ways. The speaker who runs a hot 'bath' (where the 'a' sound is pronounced like that in the word 'cat') probably lives in the north of England. The one who soaps himself in a 'barth' is likely to pay his water rates in the south. If he pronounces the 'r' in 'barth', he may well live in the west.

It should be noted, too, that accent and dialect are not simply a matter of region. Particularly in Britain, they are also a sign of social class, with the most strongly-marked features of accent (and to some extent dialect) found at the extremes of the social scale. The Royal Family, for instance, speaks an English which is 'marked up' for accent; and it tends to be easier to distinguish between speakers of different regional dialects the lower down the social scale you go.

Standards

Many believe that some English varieties are better than others. It depends, of course, on what one means by 'better': better for what purpose? The British have been notorious for the way they judge people not so much by *what* they say as *how* they say it; certain varieties carrying high social status, with others thought to be a mark of inferiority, sometimes even by the people who use them. As the writer George Orwell once remarked: 'The Englishman is branded on the tongue'.

There is still linguistic intolerance among users of English and maybe there always will be (though with the advent of the mass media, people seem more open to other ways of speaking). However, it is impossible to demonstrate objectively that any variety is more or less linguistically 'complex' or 'expressive' or 'logical' than any other. All commonly-used varieties of English are equally-developed language systems, so judgements of the better-or-worse kind are perhaps indicative more of those who make them than useful indicators of the relative qualities of one variety in terms of another.

Historically, the variety of British English which enjoyed most prestige was that used by people in the south east of England. Understandably, perhaps: London was the centre of power in the nation, the seat of royalty, Parliament and the law, church and commerce and within relatively short distances from the two major universities in the country, Oxford and Cambridge. What's more, the people who held power were also literate and so their spoken language came to be the variety which was written down. In this, it travelled through space and time, gathering the power to become the standard form. We now refer to this variety as **Standard English Dialect** ('SE'). This book describes that variety. It is also written in Standard English. If you are a non-British speaker of English, see how often you can find differences between the dialect of this book and your own standard form. It is unlikely you will find very many examples, and those you do find are not likely to be big ones.

This is not to suggest that Standard English is better than other varieties in an absolute sense. Rather it acknowledges that it is the form of English recognised the world over, the one which travels most often across regional and national boundaries, the one which is least associated with a particular social class. Indeed, Standard English is that form of the language which is characteristically used by educated speakers, which is prevalent in the media and which is preferred in writing.

Accent, too, has its standard. The accent most often associated with Standard English Dialect in Britain is known as **Received Pronunciation** ('RP'), sometimes known as 'BBC English' because of its wide use in the broadcast media. Once again, there is nothing *linguistically* virtuous in using this accent (though plenty have recognised that it may be more *socially* advantageous as they paid up for elocution lessons). That it tends to carry prestige in Britain is again largely historical. Had the centre of power in the British Isles been in York, then the people who lived in the south east would no doubt have been considered unsophisticated provincials, and the pronunciation of their quaint regional dialect would have been treated with the same amusement or disdain as, for centuries, those in London have often treated the varieties of others.

However, ask an American what he thinks of a range of British accents and dialects and he'll either not notice the difference, or confound you by preferring quite different ones from yours! It seems that, elsewhere in the English-speaking world, people have other ways of establishing social levels.

Styles

Within each variety of English, language-users may decide to adopt different *styles*, depending on the context in which the language is used. One doesn't swear at a wedding and children quickly learn that talking to Granny sometimes requires a different set of speech-rules from those used in slanging battles with the kids next door. Teenagers will have their own habits of speech (different words, ways of pronouncing, maybe even different

grammatical features) which they would not use with parents at home or with teachers at school. Listen to doctors talking, for example, or lawyers, thieves or journalists: they will have a way of conversing with each other which lay-people are not allowed to understand. Such styles help to cement the group's identity and keep it distinctive. Away from the group, however, its speakers will use a more widely-shared variety.

It is not only in speech that such variety of style occurs. Writers will try to match what they write to the expectations and needs of their readers, adopting a particular style for a specific purpose. The kind of chatty style adopted for a letter to a friend will differ from that in a learned article in a scholarly journal or a fashion review in a Sunday newspaper.

Such a style, when used to create and preserve a group or professional identity, is known as a **register**. The ability to use the right register for the purpose, and that of switching from one to another, is part of our natural fluency as adult language-users. It is a means of establishing one's credentials for belonging – another of language's social functions.

Yet whatever regional dialect or group style we adopt, ultimately our language has its own unique features which are not shared by anyone else at all. Certain ways of speaking, certain habits of the tone of voice, the accent, the pronunciation of a particular vowel, the use of an unusual word – all go to make up a personal language variety which marks out the individual rather as does a finger-print. This unique variety of an individual speaker is known technically as an **idiolect**.

No matter what language we speak, what variety of that language, what styles we may adopt in different contexts, no matter what our individual idiolect may be like, we all use a language which is constructed on the same basic principles. It will be made out of a system of sounds and written symbols which can be combined together in order to express meanings which others in the same speech community can understand. In the next chapter, we look more closely at how this process of combination – the **grammar** of language – can be described.

CHAPTER 3: GRAMMAR

Grammar is rather like electricity: we can't hear it or see it but we know it has to be there since we can experience its effects. We can hear the sounds of language and we can understand its meanings, but the way these are put together, the powerful underlying systems of connection and structure which give our language shape, are forever silent beneath its surfaces. Until we start to explore.

Functions and forms

Language has a **function** – to communicate meanings – and it has a **form** – the substance out of which those meanings are expressed linguistically. Everything we say or write must have some function (however obscure or clear, frivolous or serious, pointless or significant) and as we say or write it, we cannot avoid using its forms – its sounds or written shapes, its words, its sentence structures and so on.

There are as many functions in English as there are reasons for speaking and to describe them systematically would be very difficult, even supposing it were possible at all. (For one attempt to make such a task approachable see, for example, M. A. K. Halliday: *Explorations in the Functions of Language*, Edward Arnold, 1973.)

Describing the form is also difficult, but in this case we are helped by the fact that, even though there are many hundreds of thousands of them, the formal elements of English are not limitless in number. Neither are the many language rules which allow us to combine these elements together to make meanings.

This is a fundamental design principle of any language: that with a finite number of parts and combining-rules, we can make and understand an infinite number of different meanings. It is called **productivity**. For example, by adding the sound *ing* to a whole class of words (like *run*, *jump*, *fall*, *climb*, etc.) we allow them to join a second class of words which can be used to describe words in a third class: *running water, jumping bean, falling leaves, climbing rose*. We could even describe that productive rule by means of a simple formula:

$$\text{verb} + ing = \text{adjective}$$

You can estimate just how 'productive' this rule is when you see how often it can be applied.

The grammar of English, like that of all other languages, enables its speakers and writers to put language elements together in the *production* of an infinite number of new meanings; and, of course, their *reception* for, as possessors of this grammar, we can understand the language we hear and read as well.

Language levels

Any human language must contain three related components if people are to be able to communicate with each other.

First, there must be a **medium** in which messages are sent and received. Unless someone is reading the page aloud to you, its message is being communicated in the *visual* medium. (If the book were to be written in Braille, then of course the medium would be touch.) Most of the time, however, language operates through the medium of *sound*.

Next, there must be a **meaning** to be communicated.

Finally, there has to be some way of bringing these two together, an organisation of structural patterns which give shape and coherence to an otherwise disorganized tangle of sound and sense. These patterns, and the design-rules which make them, give language its **grammar**.

These three components of language are known as its three **levels**:

SOUND (or VISION)

⇩

GRAMMAR

⇩

MEANING

In our everyday acts of making language, the three levels are simultaneously related. To separate them like this, then, is not as obvious as may appear. Before proposing different levels in the organisation of language, linguists have had to ask: 'Can this level be disentangled intact from the rest of the fabric of the language in order to study it in isolation?' for, if not, how can it really be a separate level? The answers have sometimes led them to subdivide these levels into still further ones. For our purposes, however, they are the ones commonly agreed as being the major components of the language and we will find it useful to keep them apart like this in order to study one of them without the need to refer very often to the others.

It is not easy to imagine a language without them. Take sound or vision away and language would lack the medium through which it is expressed. Take away meaning and all we have are noise patterns or scribbles on a page – a language, perhaps, but not one we could understand, just as we can hear but may not comprehend a foreign tongue. Remove grammar and we find no language at all, but rather a haphazard stream of vocal noises and a chaos of unexpressed meanings forever held apart in incoherence.

Grammatical levels

The term **level**, already applied to language as a whole, can also be used within a description of grammar. Grammar can best be understood as a set of systems working one within the other, from high-level systems down to low-level ones. The surface of what we hear and say, read and write, consists of the most complex – high-level – grammatical elements of which language is capable. Beneath these elements, however, we find ever-smaller ones, until eventually we find ourselves examining the smallest and simplest grammatical elements of all.

These are the levels of grammar:

SENTENCE
CLAUSE
PHRASE
WORD
MORPHEME

The highest-level grammatical element is the **sentence**. Another way of putting this is to say that, in describing the structure of English, we can find no more complex element than 'sentence'. Of course, there are still bigger chunks of language (we describe them with words like 'paragraph', 'chapter', 'conversation', 'speech', 'argument', 'book', etc.) but these are not *single* elements of grammar. They are all made from a collection of sentences and part-sentences and are not themselves single structural elements any more than a building is, on its own, just one wall.

What are sentences made of? One answer is to say 'the other elements of structure'. Every sentence contains at least one **clause**; each clause is made of at least one **phrase**; each phrase contains at least one **word**; each word is made of at least one **morpheme**. Level within level within level.

In Part Two, we look at each level in turn.

PART TWO

CHAPTER 4: MORPHEMES

Take the sentence

> Three cool men stand by the shore of a threatening sea.

One way to divide it up into its component parts is to say that it consists of eleven words. However, two of those words can themselves be divided into still smaller parts. Can you identify which ones . . .?

You probably got *threatening*. It can be divided like this:

$$\rangle \text{threat} \ominus \text{en} \oslash \text{ing} \langle$$

The first part resembles a complete word which could be used in that form in many different sentences. The others, however, could never stand alone as words, though both are familiar as parts of other words: *-en* is often used at the beginning of nouns to make them into verbs, as in *encircle*, *encrust*, *enforce*, and at the end of adjectives to do the same thing: *weaken*, *brighten*, *darken*; *-ing* is used to make verbs express continuous action or to convert them into adjectives: *singing*, *falling*, *shouting*. They can even be used together: *enlivening*.

   These parts of words – {threat}, {en} and {ing} – are called **morphemes**.

   Here, then, is a productive rule of English grammar. By putting the {ing} morpheme on the ends of most verbs (as we have seen on p. 19) we can make them into adjectives. By putting the {en} morpheme on the beginnings of nouns, we make them into verbs. Other morphemes can work in a similar way. For example, by putting the {un} morpheme on the front of an adjective, we can often make it mean its opposite (*happy*, *unhappy*).

   Morphemes – conventionally shown in {curly brackets} – are the smallest elements of English grammar. Sometimes, however, they look exactly the same as words, and this can be confusing until you understand the reasons why. In our description of grammar, there are two kinds of morpheme: those – like {threat} – which can belong on their own as free-standing words, and those like {en} and {ing} which could only be found attached to such free-standing morphemes. They are called **free** and **bound** morphemes respectively.

A common mistake is to assume that words like *un-fortun[e]-ate-ly* consist of a word plus three bound morphemes. To be consistent in our description, we have to remember which level of the grammar we are examining and at the moment we are at the **morphological** level. So that word is described as consisting of the *four* morphemes:

{un} {fortune} {ate} {ly}

By the same token, the word *fortune* on its own consists of the single free morpheme {fortune}. (Notice how the spelling of such words sometimes has to alter to make room for the added morpheme, in this case with *fortune* losing its *e*: children can sometimes find this difficult to learn, *comeing* being an example of a common spelling error.)

English has many bound morphemes, a more familiar term for them being **affix**. Some go onto the ends of words and are a type of affix called a **suffix**:

happen ⊝**ing**	want ⊘**ed**
invest ⊝**ment**	wonder ⊝**ful**

Others go on the front and are called **prefixes**:

dis ⊘ similar	**un** ⊘usual
im ⊝perfect	**il** ⊝legitimate	**mis** ⊝ conduct

Find more words which include these and other affixes.

One of the longest words in the language contains a whole cluster of affixes. Can you find them all?

antidisestablishmentarianism

Which is the free morpheme and which are the bound? (Incidentally, here is a good example of the way language develops over time: *anti* and even *ism* have become common today as words in their own right – *'He's very anti anything to do with healthfoods.'* *'Here's yet another "ism" we're supposed to know all about!'* – bound morphemes becoming free.)

Some words are made by combining free morphemes:

> hope ⊖ less rail ⊖ way
> book ⊖ case cup ⊖ board

– a useful habit of English, allowing us to make new words out of old ones. Look out for others.

What do bound morphemes do? In the case of morphemes like {en} and {ing} we have seen that they serve a grammatical function, changing the grammatical status of the word to which they are affixed (for instance, from verb to adjective). They also have an important part to play in the meaning expressed. Compare the words *dog* and *dogs*. These are not totally *separate* words (since anyone who speaks English will know perfectly well that they are closely related) yet neither are they the *same* word (because it's clear that they have an important difference of meaning – a contrast signalled by the change in form). The contrast, that between singular and plural, is marked by the addition of the letter *s* in writing and the sound *z* in speech.

There are other ways, too, of expressing the same singular/ plural contrast. Common examples are:

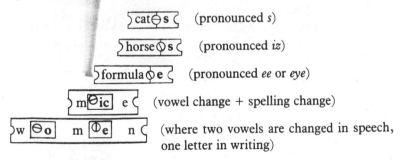

> cat ⊖ s   (pronounced *s*)

> horse ⊖ s   (pronounced *iz*)

> formula ⊖ e   (pronounced *ee* or *eye*)

> m ⊖ ic e   (vowel change + spelling change)

> w ⊖ o m ⊕ e n   (where two vowels are changed in speech, one letter in writing)

Some versions are more exotic:

> cherub ⊖ im   (pronounced *im*)

others very economical indeed:

sheep   fish   fowl   deer   (pronounced just like the singular form)

and a few even have two forms:

brother   brother∅s   br Ø̲e̲ th Ø̲ren̲

(Beware, though, of others which are not what they seem: *trousers*, for example, looks and sounds as if it is plural, but we could not easily take away the *s* to reveal the singular form. Trousers are plural already – at least at the bottom.)

All these different *forms* are realisations of the same singular/plural contrast, all examples of the same morpheme. We can call it the {plural} morpheme. All the words listed (except perhaps *trousers*) are therefore designed in exactly the same way:

{free morpheme} + {plural morpheme}

even though the forms in which this basic design is actually realised in speech or writing may differ. We learn from this that some bound morphemes, for example {plural}, can have a series of alternative realisations.

Here's one more example. Remember the sentence:

Three cool men stand by the shore of a threatening sea.

You looked earlier for *two* words which could be divided into more than one morpheme. If you couldn't before, you should by now see that *men* – {man} + {plural} – is the second.

The process of changing the form of a word in order to mark a contrast in meaning (for instance, between singular and plural) is called **inflection**. Here are some more examples:

In the two sentences:

I **call** out.
I **called** out.

the verb *call* has been inflected in the second sentence to express a different time relation from the verb in the first. Now the time is past. The same relation is expressed in the many variants on this common theme which we find in English, for instance:

I **stand** by a threatening sea.
I **stood** by a threatening sea.

28

The addition of *ed*, or the quite substantial change of sound in the second example, are both instances of the same contrast: both are examples of the {past tense} morpheme.

In the sentences:

> I **love** carrots.
> Tom **loves** peanuts.

the verb *love* in the second sentence has been inflected because it must be consistent with the noun (*Tom*) which goes before it – in this case a noun exhibiting the qualities of *3rd person* and *singular*. What's more, the tense of the verb is *present*. So the *s* added to the verb expresses in speech or writing the {3rd person, singular, present tense} morpheme.

In the sentence

> I went to **Sandra's** house.

the noun *Sandra* has been inflected with *s* because that marks the fact that she possesses the house. Hence the inflection expresses the {possessive} morpheme.

Morphology, then, is the study of the formation of words and morphemes are the elements from which those words are formed. But what has this to do with grammar? Surely, words (on their own) belong within a different level of the language: the level of *meaning*. In the case of combinations which result in new words (like *hillside*) this is true. However, we have seen from other examples that words change their shape as a result of the process of inflection. This process can happen because of pressure from elsewhere in the language environment in which the word finds its place. (The inflection of the verb to show agreement with a 3rd person singular noun is a good example of one word forcing a change of shape in another.) In such cases, we can see that morphology enters the domain of grammar – the organising systems which allow the creation of larger, more complex, linguistic elements out of smaller and simpler ones.

Where morphology restricts itself to the individual word, the combining of words together within the higher-level elements of language structure (phrases, clauses and sentences) is called

syntax. As we have seen, however, it is not always possible to separate morphology and syntax so neatly. In describing the structure of English, we are always brought face-to-face with the fact that grammar is a *set* of systems which themselves work within the wider set of systems embodying sound and meaning. So, in describing the behaviour of words as they combine together to make sentences, we must also acknowledge that some of them will be busy *internally*, changing their shapes to reflect the circumstances in which they find themselves as these sentences are created – with them and around them.

CHAPTER 5: WORDS

The vocabulary or word-stock of a language is known technically as its **lexicon**. You will see the English lexicon – or part of it – arranged alphabetically in any dictionary. Here's an example of an entry from the *The Concise Oxford Dictionary*:

> **lexical** *a*. Of the words of a language (opp. *grammatical*)

The lexicographer has alerted us to the fact that we are to understand *lexical* as being *opposed* to the word *grammatical*. Does this mean that, in any description of language, its words must be placed in an entirely separate compartment from its grammar? Not altogether, since in the same definition we see that the word is assigned a grammatical label: *a* for 'adjective'. Yet a word can only be an adjective if it is not a noun or a verb or some other kind of word, and we can only know whether it is or it isn't by seeing how it is used as part of a larger stretch of language. We need to know the context and, until we do, it is not so easy to be sure to which grammatical category a word belongs.

We saw on page 8 that we should be wary of assuming our categories are actually present in the language itself and not simply our own devices, used to help us see the language more clearly. In talking about 'verbs', 'nouns', 'adjectives', etc we should keep this in mind. Are we sure that there really are such things as 'adjectives' in the language, or is this simply a convenient label to help us remember that some words seem to behave in certain ways? Whatever the answer, at least we should try to be as rigorous as possible in using our terms. If we suspect that there is, indeed, a class of words which seem to exhibit qualities and behave in ways which allow us to collect them together into a **word-class** called 'adjective', then we must be quite clear what those qualities are. It's much too vague simply to say that 'adjectives describe things'. We need more precise tests than this. Taking our specimen word, we could for example use *syntactic* tests (in which we see how it behaves in relation to the words around it) and we could use *morphological* tests (to see whether it can take inflections like others in the word-class we think we may have discovered).

Try the tests below on the words in the panel to see whether they are what grammarians call 'adjectives' and, if so, what type of adjectives they are. For instance, *I am + well* is acceptable English (where *I am + happily* is not) so *well* must be an adjective. It passes the test which allows that any word which acceptably fills the slot in sentences made like *I + am +* [_____] fulfils the necessary requirements to be categorised as an adjective.

Some words in the list will be obvious, others less so and may leave you uncertain. If a word satisfies any one of these tests, it belongs to the word-class 'adjective' (though not all words will satisfy all the tests – suggesting that there are several different kinds of adjective).

---

quite, blue, utter, kind, upstairs, German, swimming, dead, well, sickly, poor, once, afraid, coming, sorry

---

morphological tests:

word + *ly* = adverb	(*cross – crossly*)
word + *er/est*	(*harder, hardest*)

syntactic tests:

a + word + noun	(*a sad surprise*)
very + word	(*very happy*)
I am + word	(*I am forgetful*)
more/most + word	(*more unhappy, most amused*)

Add your own words to the list and try them too.

These tests illustrate a way of discovering how words may sometimes be used within higher-level elements (phrases, clauses and sentences) while at other times they may not. It shows that words, as well as carrying meanings, are subject to the rules of grammar.

Traditionally, words lay at the heart of grammatical descriptions. The old **parts-of-speech** approach used to be the beginning, and often the end, of school grammar lessons. To identify the part of speech was called **parsing**. Such an approach attributed words to word-classes (parts-of-speech) according to their meaning. A noun, for example, was a 'naming word' while a verb was a 'doing word', adjectives were 'describing words' and adverbs 'described actions'. (Such labelling was rather more difficult however with words like *however*, *with* and *and*.)

Language seldom abides by such simple rules for long though. There are so many exceptions to the defining of words by meaning that the old labels confused more than they clarified them. How, for example, can 'doing' reside wholly in verbs when in

Sam gave him a punch

the main force of the action lies in the noun *punch*?

Nonetheless, it is important that a description of language contains some way of sorting out the words in the language as they come to be used in the higher-level elements. As you have seen, this can be done by asking questions about the functions which a word can perform within them. You know, for example, that one test for adjectives is to see whether they can fit in the empty slot in phrases like this:

a/an/the + [_____] + noun

and this little grid allows us to place any number of words in the gap and use our knowledge of the language to test whether they fit or not. Try some words in the gaps below to test whether they are adjectives.

article	adjective	noun
the	golden	throne
the	[. . .]	table
a	[. . .]	hen
the	[. . .]	song
an	[. . .]	church

So a better way to define one of the several kinds of adjective which you identified above is like this: an adjective is any word which can satisfy the structural condition that it can be used between an article and a noun, as in *the frozen lake*. And of course we can use this kind of definition for all the other word-classes in the language.

Until such tests are made, it is impossible to identify the word-class of many English words because they belong to different classes, *depending on their use*. How, for instance, can we know to which class the word *singing* belongs until we see its **function** in these sentences:

I like singing. (noun)
I'm singing. (verb)
There's a singing noise in my ears. (adjective)

(And what about

She needs a singing teacher?

Is *singing* here an adjective, or has it become part of a two-word noun: *singing teacher*?)

This puzzle poses another: is *singing* in those sentences the *same* word used in three different ways, or do we have three *different* words, each with a different meaning but sharing the same sound and spelling? The same question could be asked of *table* in the two sentences

The table seemed priceless.
The committees table amendments.

Find a dictionary and see how it handles this intriguing problem.

Open and closed

Apart from the individual word-classes (nouns, verbs, etc), the lexicon falls into one of two much broader groups as well. The main difference in meaning between the two sentences

I went into the kitchen.
I went into the bedroom.

lies in the nouns *kitchen* and *bedroom*.

Other words, however, seem to operate differently, working inside the sentence in a more functional way:

> I went into that kitchen.
> I went into this kitchen.

The words *this* and *that* have little meaning in themselves, yet they control the meaning in the whole sentence by determining the difference between the two kitchens.

The lexicon, then, seems to divide between *meaning* and *function* words, and the distinction is useful in understanding one of the design features of the language.

The distinction between meaning and function is reflected in the way the word-classes tend to fall into two groups. Those words which carry the main substance of the meaning belong to **open classes**. Each of these classes contains many thousands of items and can easily be added to as we make up new words to express new meanings. Think, for example, of the many new nouns which are now part of the language as a result of new technology: *hovercraft, microchip, hologram,* etc; and the old ones which have now been stored away in the archives: *daguerreotype, antimacassar, phrenology, groat,* etc.

There are four open classes:

> **nouns** (Tom, music, running, thought, table, ...)
> **verbs** (table, running, slow, be, do, ...)
> **adjectives** (happy, slow, thoughtful, running, ...)
> **adverbs** (then, slowly, very, afterwards, ...)

The **closed sets**, on the other hand, contain word-classes which tend to have a more functional role to play. They are much smaller than open classes and virtually static in their growth, new items being difficult to add.

There are six closed sets:

> **articles** (a[n], the)
> **determiners** (some, many, these, that, my ...)
> **pronouns** (she, I, himself, who, ...)
> **prepositions** (to, out, inside, on, against ...)
> **conjunctions** (and, but, since, because, until, ...)
> **interjections** (oh! ah! phew! ...)

Some descriptions would not separate the articles from the deter-miners. After all, one cannot use both at the same time (*my a hat*, *the some potato*). Interestingly, most of these words are also very small. In fact, there are only three open class words common in English of less than three letters: *do*, *be* and *go*.

We now know how words are constructed from morphemes and how they sometimes change their shape through the process of inflection to satisfy circumstances within the higher-level elements of phrase, clause and sentence. We also know how they function within these elements, being assigned to word-classes according to these functions. In Chapter 6, we see how words can be used to make the next element in the grammatical system – the **phrase**.

CHAPTER 6: PHRASES

Just as morphemes belong inside words, so words belong inside phrases. Phrases can be short:

$$\text{some } \mathbf{milk}$$

a bit longer:

$$\text{some more of that } \mathbf{milk}$$

or much longer still:

$$\text{some more of that really delicious } \mathbf{milk} \text{ from the local dairy}$$

In fact, there is no theoretical limit to the length of phrases. The phrase

$$\text{very, very, very } \text{cold } \mathbf{milk}$$

could go on for ever. Conversely, a phrase can be just one word long:

$$\mathbf{milk}$$

Phrase is the name given to the structural element at a level between **word** and **clause**, an empty slot in the grammatical system which we can fill with one or more words according to certain rules of grammar. That some phrases contain only one word is consistent at this level with our description of many words as containing just one morpheme at that (like the word *word* itself). Just as we have seen the inconsistency of saying that a word like *unfortunately* can consist of 'a word plus morphemes', it would be inconsistent to say that a clause could consist of 'phrases plus words' since that would be to mix up levels. Better to say that a clause consists of phrases; a phrase consists of words. No matter how many there may happen to be.

Phrases are not just *any* groups of words, of course. The grammar organises their boundaries and their internal behaviour. Try identifying the phrase-boundaries in this sentence.

All alone in her kitchen my aunt was making a little tea.

You have several possible choices in splitting this sentence into its phrases:

Was your attempt one of these? If it was the second one, you were correctly sensing the organising rules with which English grammar creates phrases.

Exploring these phrases in more detail will show us why the boundaries between them occur where they do; in other words, why they are self-contained groups of words.

my aunt and a little tea

have the same kind of structure. Each contains a noun (*aunt* and *tea*) the meaning of which is modified and made more precise by the other word or words in the phrase. The nouns themselves are essential; without them, the fundamental meaning in each phrase would vanish. We could not, for instance, make a satisfactory sentence by omitting the nouns and using the other words as substitutes:

All alone in her kitchen **my** was making **a little**

though we *can* preserve the essential meaning within the sentence if we use *only* the nouns:

All alone in her kitchen **aunt** was making **tea**

The same is true for the phrases *all alone* and *was making*. The sentence would still make sense if we removed one of the two words from each phrase. To decide which one, we could test to see what would happen to the meaning when each was omitted:

All in her kitchen my aunt was making a little tea
Alone in her kitchen my aunt was making a little tea

The adjective *alone* can be used on its own while still preserving the meaning; *all* cannot.

> All alone in her kitchen my aunt **makes** a little tea
> All alone in her kitchen my aunt **was** a little tea

Although, in the case of the verb *was making*, we will have to change its shape to make the sentence grammatical, the verb *make* in either of its inflected forms (*makes, made*) is still able to work on its own without fundamentally altering the meaning. The verb *was*, however, changes the meaning entirely.

We learn from this that some phrases are designed on the principle that a single word acts as the essential element within the phrase. We can call it the **head-word** of the phrase. (The examples on page 37 have their head-words in bold type.) All the other words in the phrase are there as subordinate elements to the head-word. (In the case of phrases like *skipping and jumping*, either *skipping* or *jumping* could act as the head-word.)

However, the same cannot be said for the phrase *in her kitchen*. If we try to leave only one word to take the place of the phrase as a whole, as we could above, we find it impossible to preserve the meaning:

> All alone **in**   my aunt was making a little tea
> All alone **her**   my aunt was making a little tea
> All alone **kitchen** my aunt was making a little tea

The two parts of that phrase – *in* and *her kitchen* – are both of equal importance and cannot work without the other being there inside the same phrase as well.

We can see from this that phrases can be split into two groups: those which operate around a head-word and those which don't.

Of the first kind, we will see that there are four types, each one gaining its identity from the word-class of the head-word. These are the **noun phrase** (*my aunt* and *a little tea*); the **verb phrase** (*was making*); the **adjective phrase** (*all alone*); and the **adverb phrase**, of which an example would be *quite slowly*.

Of the second kind, there is only one. It is introduced by a preposition and so is known as the **prepositional phrase** (*in her kitchen*). You will probably have noticed that this last example is made with a preposition followed by the noun phrase *her kitchen*: one way in which prepositional phrases are constructed.

We can now look at each type of phrase in turn:

The adjective phrase

Adjectives can occur either before the noun in a noun phrase (described on page 41):

or after certain verbs:

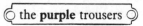

Since, in the second example, an adjective is the head-word, an adjective phrase is being used. We could make it a more complex phrase by putting an adverb in front of the head:

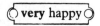

or, for emphasis, even two:

In just two cases we can put words after the head-word as well:

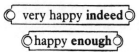

The adverb phrase

An adverb phrase may contain just one word – an adverb – as its head:

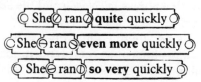

As with adjective phrases, however, we can also put other words – adverbs – before the head-word:

40

and once again we can put the words *indeed* or *enough* after the head:

It is *before* the head-word that most expansion seems to occur. It is as if, when we want to say more about an adjective or an adverb, we prefer to do so before we say the word itself.

The prepositional phrase

As its name suggests, a prepositional phrase begins with a preposition (in the *pre*-position) which is followed by a word or words which complete the phrase. It can be made in several ways: with a preposition followed by a noun phrase:

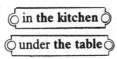

or by an adverb:

⊙ over **there** ⊙

or by an adjective:

⊙ at **best** ⊙

We can even put a preposition in front of another prepositional phrase:

⊙ over **in the field** ⊙

As we shall see in looking at the noun phrase, prepositional phrases made with a preposition + noun phrase can perform a very important function in allowing noun phrase expansion.

The noun phrase

Noun phrases have a noun as a head-word:

41

Pronouns can also act as the head-word in a noun phrase. After all, pronouns can take the place of nouns:

> **Sarah**

could become

> **She**

and even whole phrases:

> **the man in the grey suit**

could become

> **he**

In noun phrases where the head-word is a noun, there are many ways in which we can put words in front of the head. Most obviously, we can use one of the articles:

> **the** potato

or one of the determiners:

> **this** potato **my** potato **which** potato? **much** potato

You can see how determiners *determine* whether the noun acting as the head-word is countable (*those potatoes*) or whether it exists in the mass (*much potato*) or both (*this potato*).

The group before the head-word is, however, more elastic than this. We can, for instance, put words in front of the determiner:

> **another of** his potatoes

and after it:

> another of his **last** potatoes

We could also say more about the potatoes (before actually mentioning them) by using adjectives:

> another of his last **old, brown, mouldy** potatoes

42

and this process could, in theory, go on for ever. Putting words in front of the head-word in a noun phrase allows us to build up, with each word added, an ever more precise definition of the head itself.

It may be, though, that we still need to add information about the head-word *after* the event, so the noun phrase allows words afterwards as well:

the potato **over there**

the potato **over there under that table**

You can see that, in the last example, a prepositional phrase with its own noun phrase has been introduced: *under that table*. What's more, the noun *table* can have words put before it in the same way as the first head-word:

under that **old wooden** table

and after it as well:

that old wooden table **at the far end of the kitchen**

which itself contains yet two more noun phrases: *the far end* and *the kitchen*.

Here indeed is a powerful rule of grammar! A noun phrase made in this way:

[NOUN PHRASE + preposition + noun phrase + preposition + noun phrase]

allows us to construct phrases which could go on for ever. There is no theoretical limit to the length a noun phrase can be. Not surprising, when you think that there is no limit to the complexity of the places and people, objects and actions, feelings and ideas which we choose to express with them.

See if you can find the noun phrases in this piece of writing:

> She comes in her smock-frock and clogs away from the
> cool scrubbed cobbled kitchen with the Sunday-school
> pictures on the whitewashed wall and the farmers'
> almanac hung above the settle and the sides of bacon
> on the ceiling hooks, and goes down the cockleshelled

paths of that applepie kitchen garden, ducking under
the gippo's clothespegs, catching her apron on the
blackcurrant bushes, past beanrows and onion-bed and
tomatoes ripening on the wall towards the old man
playing the harmonium in the orchard, and sits down
on the grass at his side and shells the green peas that
grow up through the lap of her frock that brushes the
dew.

(extract from *Under Milk Wood* by Dylan Thomas)

The verb phrase

The verb phrase is different. Where, in the other phrases, each
new word adds something specific to the total meaning expressed,
it is harder to see the same thing happening in a verb phrase. It is
as if the whole meaning of the phrase saturates the complete
structure, making it more difficult to separate this meaning out
into its component words.

A simple verb phrase consists of just a single verb:

This verb, because it carries the main weight of meaning, is called
the **lexical verb**. It is possible to link two or more lexical verbs
together by using *and*:

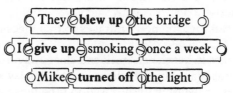

Some verbs consist of a lexical verb plus a preposition acting as an
integral part of the verb – a **verb particle**. Such verbs are known as
phrasal verbs.

Notice how some verbs made this way can be *interrupted,* for we
could just as well express those sentences like this:

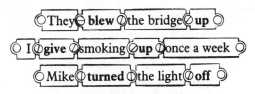

They **blew** the bridge **up**

I **give** smoking **up** once a week

Mike **turned** the light **off**

With other such verbs, this interruption is not possible:

We **come down** to the house each Sunday

could not be expressed as:

We **come** to the house **down** each Sunday

Some verbs even have two prepositions as particles:

I **catch up on** my reading at weekends

You **speak up for** all the wrong causes

A lexical verb may be inflected in certain ways to change its shape. Firstly, it may carry the {3rd person singular present tense} morpheme, which normally means adding the letter *s* to written verbs, and the sounds *s*, *z* or *iz* to spoken ones.

it **looks** he **calls** she **watches**

We have to make this inflection because of a rule – called a **concord rule** – which demands that the verb must *agree* with the noun phrase which performs its action when that noun phrase is third person singular (*he*, *she*, *one*, *it*, *Tom*, *the cat*, etc). In the case of nouns which are not third person singular, the verb must, of course, also agree – this time by *not* adding the inflection. This verb inflection provides a good example of a difference between Standard English Dialect and certain non-standard varieties. In many of the latter, there is no {3rd person singular present tense} inflection (*I call, you call, he call*), while in others it is placed on all the persons (*I calls, you calls, he calls*, etc).

In verb phrases containing only a lexical verb (or a lexical verb plus a particle), the only other inflection possible is the adding of the {past tense} morpheme: normally the letters *ed* and the sounds *d*, *t* or *id*:

She **called** I **clapped** we **doubted**

Of course, many English verbs are irregular, changing their shape in different ways to express past time; for instance:

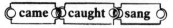
came caught sang

Notice that, when the past tense inflection is used, the {3rd person singular present tense} inflection is left out, the expression of past tense taking priority:

he **wants** she **wanted**

Tense, then, is a matter of inflection, the changing of the shape of a verb by adding (or not adding) a morpheme. You can see from this that there are only two tenses in English: **present** and **past**. Other languages may have more. French, for example, also has a **future** tense: a way of inflecting the verb (changing its shape) to express future time. English manages these things differently (see below).

We can also add other words to the lexical verb (always to the front of it). These are called **auxiliary verbs** and, together with the tense form, they are responsible for expressing, among other things, the time relation in the verb phrase.

The three most commonly used auxiliary verbs are *do*, *be* and *have* and they can occur in different forms within the verb phrase:

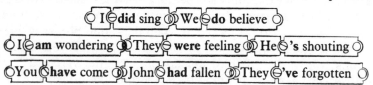
I **did** sing We **do** believe

I **am** wondering They **were** feeling He**'s** shouting

You **have** come John **had** fallen They**'ve** forgotten

With the introduction of auxiliary verbs, you can see that two further inflections become possible on the lexical verb: *ing* and *en*. The inflection *en*, as well as being used to change adjectives into verbs (as in *weaken* and *enlarge* – see page 25) acts in certain cases as an alternative {past tense} morpheme to *ed*. (This form used to be much more common in English than it is now, though occasional remnants remain today, for instance in the American English past tense of *get*, which is *gotten*.) It is also used on verbs in the **passive voice** (see page 56).

46

The *ing* ending can distinguish between a single action which occurs and then is over:

○ I ○ **take** ⊖ a pill ⊖ from the table ○

or one which is habitual:

○ I ○ **take** ○ a pill ○ every day ○

from one which is continuous:

○ I ○ **am taking** ○ pills ○ these days ○

This part of the meaning in the verb phrase is called **aspect** and because the action progresses across present time, it is **present progressive aspect**.

If we change the tense of the auxiliary verb to the past, still keeping the progressive aspect, it becomes **past progressive**:

○ I ⊖ **was taking** ⊖ the pills ○ last month ○

Another aspect – called **perfective** – contrasts with the progressive. Compare the simple past of:

○ We ○ **thought** ⊖ so ○ yesterday ○

which expresses a specified period of time, now over, with:

○ We ⊖ **have thought** ⊖ so ○ for some time ○

which expresses the fact that the action has gone on in the past and is still continuing today. This is called **present perfective aspect**.

The tense can change here as well, from present to past, and now the action, however prolonged, is definitely over:

○ We ⊖ **had thought** ○ so ○ for some time ○

This is the **past perfective aspect**.

We can even put the two aspects – progressive and perfective – together: into the **present perfect progressive** aspect:

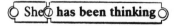
○ She ○ **has been thinking** ○

47

or into the **past perfect progressive**:

○ She⊖**had been thinking** ○

From all this, you can see that it is not easy to disentangle **aspect** from **tense**. Both are involved in expressing the moment when the action in the verb occurred, and also whether that action is over at once or continues across a period of time.

The time relation, though, is more complex still and, although the verb phrase is important in helping to express *when* something happened, the rest of the sentence can be significant as well. For example, two different times are expressed in the sentences below, yet each has the same verb phrase:

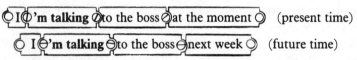

○I○**'m talking** ○to the boss○at the moment ○ (present time)

○ I⊖**'m talking** ⊖to the boss⊖next week ○ (future time)

A further enriching of meaning can be made by adding one of another group of auxiliary verbs which express a range of meanings suggesting 'probability', 'possibility', 'obligation', etc:

○He⊖**can** come○ ○I○**may** go ○

○ We○**might** fall ○○You○**mustn't** stop○

Though only a part of their meaning, these auxiliary verbs also help to indicate that an event is to occur in the future.

Auxiliaries can, of course, be used in certain combinations:

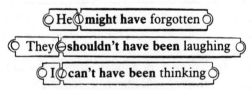

○ He○**might have** forgotten ○

○ They ⊖**shouldn't have been** laughing ○

○ I○**can't have been** thinking○

Yet another set of possibilities exists within the verb phrase. We can use another verb, followed by *to*, in front of the lexical verb:

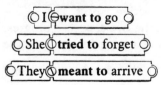

○ I ⊖**want to go** ○

○ She○**tried to** forget ○

○ They○**meant to** arrive ○

48

and these, also, can be used in combination with the others to make some very complicated structures indeed:

We should be preparing to leave

She can't have been meaning to deceive

He may have been trying to give up

Experiment with verb phrases to see what happens to the meaning when you add auxiliary verbs to the lexical verb. Try changing their order to see what is and is not allowed.

Phrases, then, are designed on one of two basic principles: those with a head-word and those without. Of the first kind, we find the noun, verb, adjective and adverb phrases, each constructed with an obligatory head-word and the optional addition of other words, before, after or each side of the head-word and subordinated to it. Of the second kind, we find the prepositional phrase in which a preposition and another element exist within the phrase in equal balance.

We have seen how, in the case of the noun phrase, limitless extension of meaning is possible because of its elastic structure, with the addition of words before and after the head. In the case of the verb phrase, we have seen that, although much more limited in size, the density of meaning can sometimes be considerable.

In the next chapter, we see what happens when phrases are put together inside the next level of grammar: the **clause**.

CHAPTER 7: CLAUSES

A **clause** is made of **clause elements**, of which one must be a verb phrase. In:

the verb phrase *likes* connects the other two elements both to itself and to each other. Without it, we would have two phrases floating apart without connection:

There may be only one other element in a clause:

or there may be more than one:

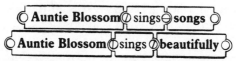

but in each case, if we remove the verb phrase, no clause can exist. So verb phrases are essential to clause construction. Clauses, then, consist of a **VERB*** element (the verb phrase) and one or more other elements, held together in a structured relationship around that VERB.

Experiment with clauses by seeing how many different ones you can make out of the collection of phrases below. Sort out the verb phrases first and note how they allow a complete structure to be constructed with other phrases. Don't worry too much about the *sense* of what the clauses say: this experiment is about struc-

---

*Note that we are now going to use the word *verb* in two senses: as a word-class and as a clause element. In the second case, it will always be written in capitals as VERB.

tures, not intelligent meanings. Feel free as well to make small alterations to words (for instance, making them singular or plural) if it will help to construct a good clause. If you want to, add your own phrases too.

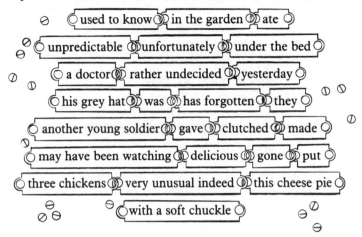

The elements of clause structure

There are seven elements of clause structure, including the VERB. The clauses you have just made should each contain a VERB and at least one other element:

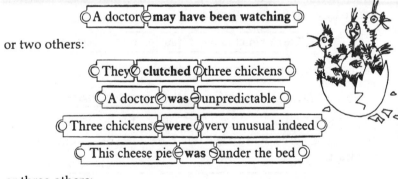

or two others:

or three others:

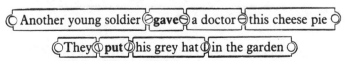

| ◯Three chickens | ◯**made** | ◯this cheese pie | ◯delicious ◯ |

or even more:

| ◯Unfortunately | ◯this grey hat | ◯**was** | ◯in the garden | ◯yesterday ◯ |

Altogether, there are seven clause elements:

> **SUBJECT (S)**
> **VERB (V)**
> **DIRECT OBJECT (O)**
> **INDIRECT OBJECT (Oi)**
> **SUBJECT COMPLEMENT (C)**
> **OBJECT COMPLEMENT (Co)**
> **ADVERBIAL (A)**

We shall look at each one in turn, first dealing with how the clause element functions within its clause – what it *does*; then at what it is made of – what it *is*.

SUBJECT

What it does in the clause

In terms of its *meaning*, the SUBJECT is normally the element which performs the action in the VERB. In terms of *clause structure*, it usually comes first in the clause:

| ◯**Three small monks** | ◯ran | ◯into the street ◯ |

but it is quite possible to put it somewhere else:

| ◯Into the street | ◯ran | ◯**three small monks**◯ |

The SUBJECT has a direct relationship with the VERB element. They must agree with each other because of a concord rule. Contrast:

| ◯**The black tower** | ◯looms | ◯against the sky◯ |

with:

| ◯ **The black towers** | ◯loom | ◯against the sky ◯ |

in which the **number** of the noun (whether it is singular or plural) affects the inflection of the verb in the VERB element.

Sometimes a clause has a **dummy subject** – a SUBJECT without a meaning. This is because the clause would be structurally incomplete without one and the dummy avoids this:

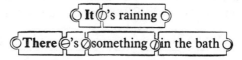

(We can show the SUBJECT is empty of meaning because we can't ask questions about it, such as: *'What's* raining?' or *'Where's* something in the bath?')

What it is made of

SUBJECTS may be made of a one-word noun phrase:

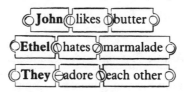

or a more complex one:

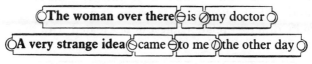

or another clause (see Chapter 8).

VERB

What it does in the clause

In terms of its *meaning,* the VERB element expresses the action performed by the SUBJECT. The 'action' may not, however, be particularly active, being sometimes more a matter of *being* or *feeling* or *becoming* – states of existence – rather than performed actions like *singing* and *dancing.* You can see the contrast in:

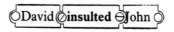

○ John ⊙ felt ⊘ slightly insulted ○

In terms of *clause structure*, the VERB is, as you have found out, the crucial element since, without it, there could be no clause at all. It establishes a relationship between itself, the SUBJECT and the remaining clause elements. This relationship will differ as a result of the different kinds of VERB element being used. In the clause:

○ Auntie Blossom ⊙ **was** ⊖ a very old lady ○

the VERB expresses the fact that Auntie Blossom and the very old lady are the same person: the SUBJECT *is* the element following the VERB. Such a relationship is an **intensive** one: that is, one in which two elements are connected because they refer to the same thing. It is made possible by the VERB (the element which makes this connection) and hence VERBS of this kind are called **intensive verbs**.

Similarly, the SUBJECT can *feel* or *become* the element following the VERB:

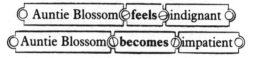
○ Auntie Blossom ⊙ **feels** ⊖ indignant ○

○ Auntie Blossom ⊙ **becomes** ⊘ impatient ○

where once again the relationship is intensive, the two elements around the VERB referring to the same thing.

A quite different relationship can be created with the clause if another kind of VERB is used:

○ Auntie Blossom ○ **tried to avoid** ○ a very old lady ○

Here, the SUBJECT *does something* to the third element. Such a relation is called **extensive**, the VERB being an **extensive verb**.

The distinction between intensive and extensive relationships is important: it shows us that there is more than one kind of VERB and hence more than one kind of clause.

Of course, we can make clauses which don't have a third element at all, clauses like:

○ The solution ⊙ **emerged** ○

Clauses like these, with only a SUBJECT (S) and a VERB (V), are the most basic kind of clause in the language. They are called **SV** structures and are made possible by using a verb which need not be related to any other element except its SUBJECT. Such verbs are called **intransitive verbs**.

By contrast, those extensive verbs which may take another element as well as the SUBJECT are called **transitive verbs**:

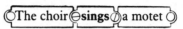

We should remember, though, that most verbs can be used both transitively and intransitively:

So the VERB element is crucial in forming the clause and there are different kinds of VERB element (depending on the verb phrase used) making possible different kinds of clause. Though a special relationship exists between the VERB and its SUBJECT, we have not yet seen how the other clause elements relate to the VERB. However, it should be clear by now that they will gain their identity within the whole clause as a result of the kind of VERB being employed.

What it is made of

The VERB element is made of either a simple, one-word, verb phrase:

or a complex one:

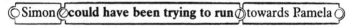

DIRECT OBJECT

What it does in the clause

Some clauses are made of a SUBJECT, a transitive VERB and a third element:

This third element is the DIRECT OBJECT (O) and such clauses can be called **SVO** structures.

In terms of its *meaning*, the SUBJECT (the 'actor') typically does something (the 'action') to an OBJECT.

In terms of *clause structure*, the DIRECT OBJECT achieves its identity because of its position relative to the VERB. For example, we could reverse the elements in that clause:

and the DIRECT OBJECT would then be *my big sister*.

The kind of clauses illustrated so far have been made in the **active voice**, that is: clauses in which the SUBJECT is the actor of the action in the VERB. SVO clauses, however, can also be transformed from the active into the **passive voice**. This is a different kind of structure, equivalent in meaning but with the actor of the VERB moved from its role as the SUBJECT, and the OBJECT of the action moved to the SUBJECT position. Contrast:

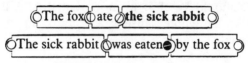

The meanings are identical. In the second clause, the SUBJECT of the first (*the fox*) is at the end of the clause and the DIRECT OBJECT (*the sick rabbit*) has moved to SUBJECT position. The preposition *by* has also been introduced and the verb has been inflected with the {en} morpheme. So we find that passive clauses are those in which the 'actor' of the action in the VERB, becomes the 'agent' of the action in the equivalent passive structure, while the OBJECT of that action becomes the grammatical SUBJECT of the passive clause. (Not surprisingly, children can sometimes find it a little confusing to understand passive clauses.) Note that we cannot make the same active/passive equivalents out of clauses made with intensive verbs:

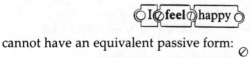

cannot have an equivalent passive form:

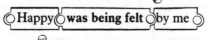

so in some cases this is another way to distinguish between extensive and intensive structures.

What it is made of

A DIRECT OBJECT can just as well be the SUBJECT if we move it to the other side of the VERB. So, like that element, it too consists of a noun phrase. It may also consist of a clause (see Chapter 8).

SUBJECT COMPLEMENT

What it does in the clause

In terms of its *meaning*, the SUBJECT COMPLEMENT says what the SUBJECT is, or is feeling, becoming, seeming, etc.

In terms of *clause structure*, we need once again to look at the VERB. Just as an extensive verb can result in a clause having a DIRECT OBJECT, so the SUBJECT COMPLEMENT (C) finds its place in the clause as the result of an intensive verb. The most common of these verbs is *be* – a kind of linguistic = (or ≠) sign

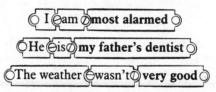

and the clauses they make are known as **SVC** structures, the third element being the SUBJECT COMPLEMENT.

What it is made of

There are two kinds of SUBJECT COMPLEMENT normal in SVC clauses. One, as with the SUBJECT or the DIRECT OBJECT, is a noun phrase:

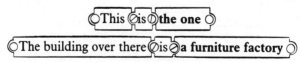

The second kind is an adjective phrase:

○ She ○ wasn't ○ **quick enough** ○

It can also be a clause (see Chapter 8).

INDIRECT OBJECT

What it does in the clause

In terms of the *meaning* of the clause:

○ I ○ gave ⊖ **Tom** ⊖ a piece of my mind ○

we find a DIRECT OBJECT (*a piece of my mind*) which is given to a recipient (*Tom*). The recipient is the INDIRECT OBJECT (Oi) and such clauses are known as **SVOO** structures.

In terms of *clause structure*, the INDIRECT OBJECT is made necessary, as are other kinds of clause, by the nature of the VERB. This time, it allows *two* objects to be used within the clause.

It is not possible to have a clause with only a SUBJECT, VERB and INDIRECT OBJECT. This would result in clauses like:

○ I ○ gave ⊖ **Tom** ○

and although, out of context, it is unlikely we would ever use such a structure, it is easy to imagine a context in which this would become a perfectly understandable SVO clause:

> I had two kittens called Tom and Tim. I wanted to give one of them away so **I gave Tom.**

Clauses with INDIRECT OBJECTS may have *two* passive equivalents:

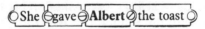
○ She ○ gave ⊖ **Albert** ⊘ the toast ○

can transform to either:

○ Albert ○ was given ⊘ the toast ● by her ○

or:

○ The toast ○ was given ○ to Albert ● by her ○

and the final element (*by her*) is, of course, optional.

What it is made of

Like the DIRECT OBJECT, an INDIRECT OBJECT consists of a noun phrase, or a clause (see Chapter 8).

OBJECT COMPLEMENT

What it does in the clause

In terms of its *meaning*, this one is fairly hard to describe. The OBJECT COMPLEMENT (Co) is what someone or something is or becomes as a result of an action performed by someone or something else. Well – look at the example then:

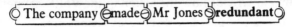

The SUBJECT (*The company*) performs an action in the VERB (*made*) which causes the DIRECT OBJECT (*Mr Jones*) to be, or to become, something else (*redundant*); *redundant* is the OBJECT COMPLEMENT. Such clauses are called **SVOC** structures.

In terms of *clause structure*, it is possible to think of clauses like this as being made up from two others:

which come together rather like this:

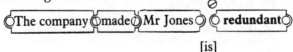

Once again, it is the VERB element which allows this to happen. Verbs like *make* can be complicated in their effects within the clause. You can see that, in this case, the VERB not only distinguishes the DIRECT OBJECT from the SUBJECT (because of their relative positions) but also the DIRECT OBJECT from the OBJECT COMPLEMENT.

What it is made of

Like the SUBJECT COMPLEMENT, an OBJECT COMPLEMENT can be made of a noun phrase:

The committee elected Mr Smith president

or an adjective phrase:

The music made them sad

or a clause (see Chapter 8).

ADVERBIAL

What it does in the clause

In terms of its *meaning*, the ADVERBIAL (A) generally tells us where, when, why or how the action in the VERB happened.

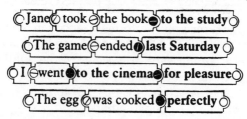

Jane took the book to the study

The game ended last Saturday

I went to the cinema for pleasure

The egg was cooked perfectly

It can also tell us something about the attitude of the speaker:

Unfortunately I can't stand doughnuts

An interesting development in English has happened recently in the use of the word *hopefully*.

Hopefully I'll be there tomorrow

has come to mean that the speaker hopes he will be there tomorrow. He is not commenting on the state of mind he is in as he makes this statement. Nor is he saying in what state of mind he will be when he arrives. Contrast this with:

I'll be there tomorrow full of hope

and we can see an example of how language changes over time.

An ADVERBIAL can also make a connection – perhaps of order – with a prior clause:

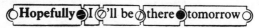

Secondly I should like to thank the catering staff

60

It can also signal logical connections with clauses which have gone before:

In terms of *clause structure*, certain kinds of clause demand the use of an ADVERBIAL. The first type uses an intensive verb to create **SVA** structures:

Such clauses express location. Sometimes, though, this location is metaphorical:

and we're back to expressing states of being (like *I feel happy*). Such clauses, then, are very like certain SVC structures in meaning.

The second type uses a VERB resulting in a clause which must have both a DIRECT OBJECT and an ADVERBIAL to be complete:

Such clauses are known as **SVOA** structures.

Apart from these compulsory uses of the ADVERBIAL, this clause element differs from the others in that it may be omitted from a clause without creating a faulty structure. It is also the most mobile, occurring in most places within the clause; at the beginning:

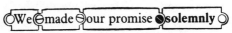

in the middle:

We solemnly made our promise

or at the end:

We made our promise solemnly

and though all the other elements may only occur once within any clause, there is no theoretical limit to the number of ADVERBIALS which a clause may contain:

> **On Monday,** a blackbird **in the garden** was **gently** preening itself **in the sunshine, like a dark angel.**

What it is made of

ADVERBIALS are made of one-word adverb phrases:

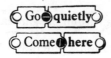

or more complex ones:

They can also be prepositional phrases:

In the last case, there is an equivalence of meaning, though not of structure, with SVOO clauses (*The pupils gave their teacher a present*). It can also be made of another clause (see Chapter 8).

It should be clear by now that there is no difference between a clause and certain kinds of sentence. Why then have clauses at all? Why not go straight from **phrase** to **sentence** in our description, without this intervening level?

The answer is that it can be useful to keep **clause** in the description since, as we shall see in the next chapter, some clauses cannot stand on their own as sentences, unlike those in the examples above. Furthermore, sentences can contain more than one clause and to describe them without reference to the clauses they contain would force us to have to say, 'A sentence can consist of more than one sentence.' This would not be sensible.

Now we have arrived at **sentence**, we will have to introduce three new terms into the description: **simple**, **compound** and

complex. **Simple sentences** contain only a single clause (like the ones in this chapter). **Compound sentences**, on the other hand, contain two or more clauses, joined in a chain, one next to the other. **Complex sentences** also contain more than one clause, but they are joined in different kinds of ways.

In the next chapter, we look at the ways in which English grammar allows us to put clauses together to make its most complex element: the **sentence**.

CHAPTER 8: SENTENCES

Sentences are the most complex complete elements we can find in the grammar of English. The study of their shapes and behaviour is called **syntax**. They are made as a result of combining together elements from the levels we have already explored: the words and their component morphemes; the phrases with their words; the clauses with their phrases. Sentences contain clauses (and so all those other elements as well). We have seen that some – **simple sentences** – contain only a single clause (and that, therefore, there is no difference between them). Others, however, contain more than one clause, and much of the grammar of sentence structure is concerned with the systems of connection which allow clauses to be joined together.

Some say sentences exist only in written language. They argue that features common in speech (like *um* and *er* and the many false starts, repetitions and hesitations we all make when we speak) are absent from writing and that therefore we cannot really call them parts of sentences. They belong, they argue, *outside* the grammatical system. Others will reply that, despite these features (which in any case have been shown to be rather more systematic than people once thought), spoken language displays a sufficient number of sentence features to make 'sentence' a legitimate element of grammar in both speech and writing.

Sentences are made because the grammatical rules which generate them are **productive**, allowing an infinite number of unique structures to be created from the comparatively limited set of structural frames available within the grammar. We have seen already that there are only seven elements of clause structure, yet out of those seven, any number of simple sentences can be made. The same is true for all sentences, though now we have the added possibilities of putting clauses together – which, of course, greatly adds to the complexity of the structures we can make (and therefore to the meanings we can map onto them).

Minor sentences

Before looking at the range of possibilities these productive rules offer in making sentences, we need first to consider a small group of sentences which are the exceptions to them. These are *not* productive. They are, though, very common. They are known as **minor sentences**. They tend to have ready-made shapes which seldom change and which are not easy to describe in the same way as all other sentences in the language.

Some of them are used as responses:

> Yes.   No.   Sorry!   Pardon?   Please.

Others are used as social utterances:

> Hello.   Goodbye.   How d'you do?

Some are normally only found on written notices:

NO ENTRY   LADIES   CHAPTER TWO   KEEP OFF THE GRASS

Some are *formula* sentences in which the basic shape is laid down and the language-user simply adds the appropriate parts to suit the occasion:

> Long live the . . .!
>
> Down with . . .!
>
> To hell with . . .!

Add your own to these examples.

Major sentences

By contrast, we know all other sentences as **major sentences,** no matter whether they contain one or more than one clause. Unlike minor sentences, which are ready-made structures, major sentences are limitless in number because of the productivity of the rules which generate them. We make them up and hear or read other people's all the time. Using the elements of clause structure and the rules of grammar, we can produce and understand an infinite number of them. For instance, apart from the quoted examples (morphemes, words, phrases, minor sentences, and its headings and sub-headings, etc), this book is made entirely of major sentences. Each one different.

Any serious examination of language, then, will need to look carefully at the way major sentences come to be constructed for the methods of construction lie at the heart of human language.

Sentence categories

There are four basic categories of major sentence in English:

> **statements**
> **commands**
> **exclamations**
> **questions**

Each type has different structural features, though these differences may seem comparatively small. Our description will concentrate mainly (as it did in the last chapter) on **statements** – by far the most common category. However, for the sake of completeness, here are some examples of each type with some of their structural features pointed out:

Statements

> My best friend leaves the room

Contrast the examples below with this kind of structure, in which the SUBJECT – *my best friend* – is followed by a VERB – *leaves* – and then by the rest of the sentence.

Commands

> Leave the room

Here the SUBJECT – *you* – has been omitted from the statement: [*You*] *leave the room*.

> Let's leave the room

Here the verb *let* is introduced with a first person plural SUBJECT – *us* (contracted to *'s*) – which has been moved to the other side of this verb.

66

Exclamations

> What a tactless thing to do!

Here *what* (a WH-word found also in questions) has been introduced in place of *it was* in the equivalent statement.

> How tactless!

Here another WH-word – *how* – has been put in place of *it was*, followed by an adjective. Notice the relatedness of structure between the question:

> How tactless was it?

and the exclamation:

> How tactless it was!

Questions

a) 'Yes/No' type
(because they expect a 'yes-or-no' answer):

> Did your best friend leave the room?

Here the auxiliary verb *did* has been swapped to the other side of the SUBJECT *your best friend*, so making a statement into a question.

b) 'WH' type
(because a WH-word – *what, when, who, why, where, how,* etc – signals the need for further information):

> Who left the room?
> Where did your best friend go?
> Why did your best friend leave the room?

Here, apart from the introduction of the WH-word and, in two cases, the auxiliary verb *did*, the order of elements in the sentences has been reorganised from the equivalent statement forms. These statement forms are likely to emerge in the replies:

> X left the room
> My best friend went – to X
> My best friend left the room – because X

c) 'Either/or' type

(because an alternative answer is possible):

> Was it your best friend who left the room or his brother?

Here the auxiliary *was* has been swapped around its dummy SUBJECT *it* and the word *or* has been introduced.

d) 'Tag' type

(because a statement has been made into a question by adding a 'tag'):

> It wasn't your best friend who left the room, was it?
> It was your best friend who left the room, wasn't it?
> Your best friend left the room, didn't he?
> Your best friend didn't leave the room, did he?

Here the tag is made of an auxiliary verb + SUBJECT. Note how positive statements are followed by negative tags, and vice versa.

Joining clauses

Simple sentences contain a single clause, but it is possible to make sentences which contain more than one. How many ways can you join these simple sentences together to make ones with more than a single clause? Feel free to make small changes (in the words and their order) if it will help to make a good join.

> I used to want to go sailing.
> I could never afford a boat.
> Last summer I received a letter from a solicitor.
> I had been left some money by a distant relative.
> The relative had died.
> Immediately, I joined a sailing club.
> I found out about different kinds of boats there.
> Now I'm much better informed.
> I'll probably buy a boat next week.

There are many ways to make the joins. Perhaps you put them all into one big sentence by joining each clause with a word like *and*. Alternatively, you may have used other words to put two clauses together:

> I used to want to go sailing **although** I could never afford a boat.

even swapping the order of those two clauses:

> Although I could never afford a boat, I used to want to go sailing.

You might have joined two of the clauses into one like this:

> I had been left money by a distant relative **who had died**.

or even squeezed the whole of the last clause into one adjective:

> I had been left money by a distant **dead** relative.

Perhaps you came up with a solution like this for two of the clauses:

> Immediately I joined a sailing club **where** I found out about different kinds of boats.

or even one of these two:

> Immediately I joined a sailing club, **finding out** about different kinds of boats there.

> Immediately I joined a sailing club **to find out** about different kinds of boats.

Again, the second of these joins would have allowed you to change the order of clauses:

> To find out about different kinds of boats, I joined a sailing club immediately.

This capacity of the language to combine elements together is crucial in explaining its creative potential. The ways in which clauses may be joined demonstrates something of the beauty and the power of the grammatical systems we find in our language. What follows begins from the perception that clauses can be joined in one of two ways: they can be put *next to each other* or *one inside the other*.

Compound sentences

The simplest way to join clauses is to put them next to each other, using a joining-word to cement them into a larger, single, unit:

I like coffee ⊕ **and** ⊕ my friend likes tea

Sentences in which two or more clauses are joined next to each other like this are known as **compound sentences**. Each clause is structurally of equal weight with the others within the sentence, like scales in perfect balance: **co-ordinated**.

This particular compound sentence is made possible by the use of the joining-word *and*. The technical term for such words is **conjunction**. Three conjunctions – *and*, *but* and *or* – allow clauses to be put *next to* each other. They are called **co-ordinating conjunctions** (**co-ordinators** for short).

The pilot sneezed ⊕ **and** ⊕ the plane went into a nose-dive

I used to like Enid Blyton ⊗ **but** ⊗ now I prefer Proust

He looks angry ⊗ **but** ⊗ he may be pretending

We could go for a walk ⊗ **or** ⊗ we could watch the television

Compound sentences can, of course, be made with any number of clauses and with all three conjunctions:

> Sarah was tired **and** she obviously needed a weekend in the country **or** at least she needed a day in bed with a good book **but** she was determined to go to the interview.

Complex sentences

The second way of joining sentences is more complicated. It is called **subordination**. In this process, clauses are put together *one inside the other* to make what are called **complex sentences**.

The best way to see what it means to put one clause inside another is to start with a simple (one-clause) sentence and work up from that.

○ **On Saturday** ●I ⊖went○ to a football match ○

      A   S V   A

The first ADVERBIAL (*On Saturday*) here consists of a pre-positional phrase. However, if we change the phrase to:

When I finished work ●I ⊖went○ to a football match ○

the ADVERBIAL element of the clause *I went to a football match* is itself a clause. This makes the resulting sentence a complex sentence, with an ADVERBIAL element which can, in turn, be unpacked to reveal its own elements of clause structure:

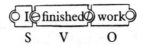

$$S \quad V \quad O$$

We can show this happening more clearly like this:

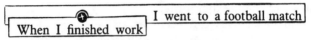

It should be clear that the lower clause (*I finished work*) has been joined to the higher clause (*I went to the football match*) by putting it inside the resulting complex sentence as an ADVERBIAL element. Thus the **subordinate clause** (in this case an ADVERBIAL) is *When I finished work*.

The join is made possible because of *when*, the **subordinating conjunction** (or **subordinator**). It achieves a comparable function to the co-ordinating conjunctions in compound sentences but this time *sub*ordinates its clause to the clause above it. If we took it away, we should have two simple sentences, in written language showing their separation with a full-stop and, in speech, by an intonation signal like a drop in voice-pitch after the first sentence:

| I finished work. | I went to a football match. |

If you aren't yet sure of the difference between subordination and co-ordination, try this test: in a complex sentence, the subordinate clause can sometimes move to a different position without changing the overall meaning. For instance, the sentence above could just as well be expressed as:

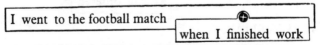

Note that the subordinator travels with its clause, or the meaning – and the subordinate clause – would have to change:

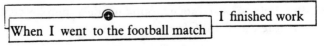

However, in a compound sentence, this ability to move clauses doesn't apply:

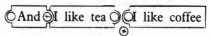

cannot become

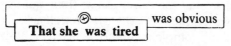

All we could do would be to swap the two clauses round the pivotal *and* to change their order.

Subordinate clauses can occur as any element of the clause above it – except, of course, the VERB itself. As SUBJECT:

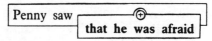

as DIRECT OBJECT:

Penny saw **that he was afraid**

as INDIRECT OBJECT:

My Dad gave **whoever it was** the last biscuit

as SUBJECT COMPLEMENT:

It isn't **what I wanted**

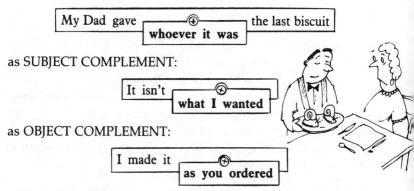

as OBJECT COMPLEMENT:

I made it **as you ordered**

and as ADVERBIAL:

I love you **because you have lovely thoughts**

Subordinate clauses can move around inside a complex sentence, coming before the SUBJECT:

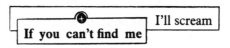

or after the VERB:

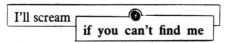

We can go still further, embedding a subordinate clause inside a subordinate clause to make complex sentences with multiple levels of structure:

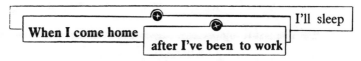

These sentence-joining systems can, of course, work together. We can make complex sentences in which co-ordinated clauses contain subordinate clauses within them:

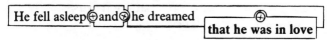

or the other way round, with a subordinate clause containing two or more co-ordinated clauses:

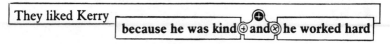

Go back to your sentence-joining activity on page 68. How many of the joining processes above did you make use of?

The relative clause

An important variety of subordinate clause is one in which not all but only a part of the higher-level clause element contains a subordinate clause:

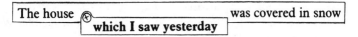

Here, the SUBJECT noun phrase (*the house*) has been augmented by the subordinate clause *which I saw yesterday*. This is a very common form of subordination, so much so that it has its own label: **relative clause**. The subordinator (*which*) similarly has a label: the **relative pronoun**.

Here are some more examples of relative clauses:

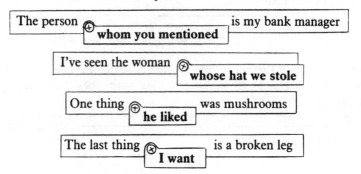

The person ⊕ whom you mentioned is my bank manager

I've seen the woman ⊗ whose hat we stole

One thing ⊕ he liked was mushrooms

The last thing ⊗ I want is a broken leg

In the last two examples, the relative pronouns have been left out: a common feature of the relative clause. See **ellipsis** below.

This kind of subordinate clause provides us with an interesting case of linguistic ambiguity, one that often causes problems with punctuation. The two sentences

> The girl who was wearing a blue dress was crying.
> The girl, who was wearing a blue dress, was crying.

both have exactly the same structure, with a relative clause embedded within the SUBJECT element of the clause above it. However, they express different meanings. In the first, the relative clause serves the function of distinguishing the girl from any other girl we may want to talk about:

> **The girl who was wearing a blue dress** was crying but the one in the red bikini was having a sensational time.

In the second sentence, however, the fact that the girl was wearing a blue dress is added for no other reason than to give us a piece of extra information. It is put between commas in written language, and would be isolated by intonation features in speech, in order to show that it is not crucially connected to the noun phrase *the girl*, as it is in the first sentence.

Where the relative clause restricts the meaning to a particular noun phrase, as it does in the first example, it is called a **restrictive relative clause**; where it does not restrict the meaning, but simply adds further information, it is called a **non-restrictive relative clause**.

Finite and non-finite

We cannot leave the subordinate clause without noting another kind of subordination. This uses a different method of signalling the join between the subordinate clause and the one – the **superordinate clause** – of which it forms a component element. It depends on the state of the VERB element, since it is the VERB which controls the clause in which it finds itself.

Verbs can take either a **finite** or a **non-finite** form (see the examples below). Depending on which of these forms it takes will be the state of the clause in which it is used. A verb in its finite state will form a **finite clause**; in its non-finite state, a **non-finite clause**. Non-finite clauses are another type of subordinate clause.

A finite verb can belong inside a clause which may stand on its own as a simple sentence:

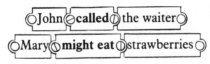

A non-finite verb, however, could *not* allow a simple sentence to be formed:

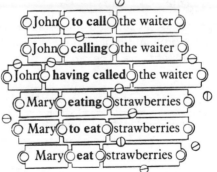

However, such non-finite clauses could all be used as subordinate clauses in complex sentences:

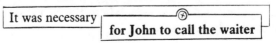

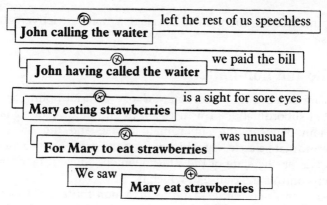

A subordinate clause, then, can be either finite or non-finite depending on the state of its VERB. The superordinate clause, however, must be governed by a verb in its finite state. It can be helpful to call this VERB the **main verb** to distinguish it from any other VERB within the sentence.

Leaving things out

You have already seen that in some relative clauses we may leave out the relative pronoun:

The book [which] I read yesterday has changed my life

Leaving things out is, in fact, an important process in English grammar. It saves time and tidies up what would otherwise be a language full of repetitions. The process is called **ellipsis**. For example, in:

Mrs Meed went to Mayfair and Mrs Meed bought a hotel

we don't really need – and certainly wouldn't say – the words *Mrs Meed* in the second clause. A more natural way of putting it would be:

Mrs Meed went to Mayfair and bought a hotel

The process of ellipsis is commonly found in the second or subsequent clauses of sentences where the SUBJECT of the first clause has already been said:

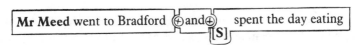

A half-way measure is to squeeze the words *Mr Meed* into the pronoun *he*.

It is not only the SUBJECT which is left out. In sentences where the VERB contains auxiliaries, these too may be omitted in subsequent clauses:

Ellipsis raises an interesting problem of grammatical description. In co-ordinated structures like *singing and dancing*, we have a choice of analysis. In the sentence

we may either choose to describe the sentence as SVA [SUBJECT: *She*; VERB: *was singing and dancing* (a co-ordinated structure with two heads); ADVERBIAL: *all night*) or like this:

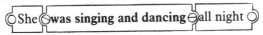

Especially in conversations like the one below, we can even omit clause elements, leaving the sentence with only a single one:

> A: When are you going to Manchester?
> B: On Monday.

where B's reply elides the SUBJECT (*I*), the VERB (*am going*) and the ADVERBIAL (*to Manchester*) and leaves only the ADVERBIAL necessary to answering the question: *on Monday*.

Ellipsis can also occur in another way in some subordinate clauses, for they contain no verb at all. Somewhere in the past history of the clause, however, we can still find evidence of a vanished structure which is not unlike a full clause, its VERB intact:

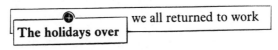

Here, we can easily imagine the non-finite verb *being* making this into a non-finite clause acting as an ADVERBIAL in the sentence:

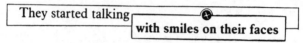

In the next example, the verb *were* seems to have been left out:

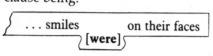

the lost finite clause being:

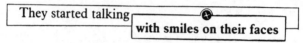

Clauses like these, in which the VERB has been omitted through ellipsis, are called **verbless clauses**.

To describe the structure of English sentences in exhaustive detail would, of course, take up a great deal more space than this. There are many, many more rules of grammar and a host of different structural features which we have no room for in a book like this. Here, however, are the main structural patterns of sentences and some of the rules which allow them to be generated. People who speak English share them all, inside their heads as part of their language and outside in the community of language-sharers who make up the English-speaking world.

Other languages, too, will have their own grammars – no less complex and powerful, no less elastic and intricate, than this one. The ability to make sentences is, after all, one of the most fundamental of all human capacities.

However, there is more to making language than simply putting sentences together in their component parts. In the final chapter, we look briefly at some of the things which happen **beyond grammar**.

CHAPTER 9:
BEYOND GRAMMAR

The grammar described in this book will allow us to construct a limitless number of sentences, the frames onto which we can place the infinity of individual meanings which we use English to make. On its own, however, it will not allow us to build those stretches of language *longer* than a sentence of which, most of the time, language consists. The grammar described here is not designed for the purpose. There is more to come – further descriptions which are only partly concerned with grammar and which contain other parts, different rules of connection, additional systems.

Discourse

Stretches of language longer than a sentence are called **discourse** and, like sentences, they also have systems which bind them together and give them shape and unity between their boundaries. (How otherwise would we know where one piece of language ends and a new one begins?)

There are many forms which discourse may take, different kinds having varying patterns which, to a greater or lesser extent, are subject to rules of structure. Some, like a wedding ceremony or a funeral service, have unbending rules, their forms being written down, and altered in each new realisation only in the names of the participants concerned. Others, like conversations between friends over a drink, have much looser structures, ones harder to describe explicitly. However, the study of discourse – **discourse analysis** – seeks to discover the principles of construction in even these apparently formless examples of language, approaching the task on the assumption that such laws must be there if the discourse is to be possible at all. Perhaps there is a 'grammar' of chunks of language larger than a sentence, one which helps us to sustain discourses with other people as well as to make those which – like this book – contain only a single voice.

The very discourse of this book assumes certain shared rules and conventions, elements of common ground with its readers without which it would be largely incoherent. In writing it, the author has had to make assumptions (that the reader is literate, is intelligent, is prepared to think, wants to discover something, will ask questions, won't be content with this as the whole story, knows how to go and find information from elsewhere, etc) because, without such assumptions, there would be no point in trying to explain English grammar in a book at all. He is also assuming that some people will *not* need this book because they already know what it has to say. They are further advanced in the discourse of talking and writing about language, having a more sophisticated metalanguage than the one this book attempts to explore. Had it been written for such readers, the kind of discourse features it exhibits might have differed (much more technical language, for instance; a far greater insistence on exceptions and ambiguities; less explanatory commentary; fewer paragraphs like this one). Discourse is chunks of language made between people, and that must include those partners in the discourse who remain for the most part silent.

To understand this is to raise important questions about education (and so, in the end, about the nature of our civilisation). As a child grows to maturity, it becomes increasingly active within the linguistic behaviour of the surrounding world (domestic in the home; local in the community; national and international through the media; and exploratory in its ranging across new processes and areas of knowledge in the school). To enter into this linguistic community, the child needs more than simply morphemes, words, phrases, clauses and sentences. By the time it becomes an adult, the need will be for that bottomless collection of language rules which will allow full participation in events for which discourse becomes a social, intellectual and emotional imperative.

A child new to reading, for instance, may find the fact that pages like this are segmented into paragraphs puzzling: the discourse rule which organises written language in this way is one it has yet to learn. Years later, as it studies for public examinations, much of its effort will be directed not simply to acquiring new facts, ideas, processes and skills, but to learning how to enter the particular discourses of the subjects concerned. Learning a subject is, in part at least, learning to be at home with the language in which a person has their existence. Take that away and the subject ceases to exist.

The process of making discourse seems to begin very early indeed, as the infant and the parent speak together – first one, then the other, then the first again – the child learning one of the primary discourse rules: that we (usually) take it in turns to do the talking. Imagine the range and sophistication of discourse rules which, as adults, we have learned since then: rules which help us through job interviews and courtships, dinner parties and tea with grandparents, club outings and trips to the doctor, telephone calls and shopping expeditions, mornings in the office and evenings in the pub. And then there are the rules of discourse which we use when reading and writing . . .

Cohesion

Essential to the making of discourse is the capacity of language to connect *across* sentence boundaries. Such behaviour is known as **cohesion**. It works in many ways. Take, as an example, the word *it* which began the last sentence. It referred to a particular word – *cohesion* – which had already been used in the sentence before. This illustrates one system of cohesion, known as **reference** because it displays language's ability to *refer* from one part of the discourse to another. Here is a fuller example:

1. Yesterday, Laura and her husband went to buy a picture.
2. In the little gallery above a restaurant in the centre of town, they browsed among the water colours by local

artists, the small oil sketches of poppies and primroses, the bold landscapes and the chaste interiors.

3. He suggested they buy a finely-detailed study of rocks on the crest of a dark hillside.

4. Her preference, however, was for the flowing lines of a lithograph showing a local church.

5. They spent an hour there in pleasant disagreement.

6. He wanted to postpone a decision until another day.

7. She didn't.

8. Eventually, they both decided on a small hand-coloured etching of trees against a winter sunset.

9. She proposed that they go to buy another picture at the local Art Society exhibition on Saturday.

10. He didn't want to do so as they had spent too much money already.

They in sentences 2, 3, 5, 8, 9 and 10 refers to *Laura and her husband* in sentence 1, as does *both* in sentence 8. *He* in sentences 3, 6 and 10 refers to *her husband,* and *Her* in sentences 1 and 4 refers to *Laura,* as does *she* in sentences 7 and 9. *There* in sentence 5 has as its **referent** *the little gallery above a restaurant in the centre of town* in sentence 2. *Didn't* in sentence 7 refers to *wanted to postpone* in sentence 6. *So* in sentence 10 refers to *go to buy another picture at the local Art Society Exhibition on Saturday* in sentence 9.

This pattern of words – **reference items** – which are threaded through the discourse helps to give it shape and unity by establishing a web of connection from one part to another.

The word *the* plays an important part as well in making the discourse: *the water colours . . . the small oil sketches . . . the bold landscapes* (sentence 2) imply that we, the readers, *know* what kind of paintings these are; have been to just such a gallery and know what to expect. The writer does not anticipate that the reader will ask 'Which?' in each case. The same thing happens with *the little gallery* (sentence 2), *the flowing lines . . .* (sentence 4) and *the local Art Society* (sentence 9): it is part of the way this discourse works that such specification helps us to feel we know the kind of things being described. Contrast this with the uses of *a* in sentences 3, 4 and 8.

Other words, too, achieve cohesion. The discourse is placed in time by the words *yesterday* (sentence 1) and *on Saturday* (sentence 9) so that we are aware of the overall context of time in which the incident takes place. (Contrast the vaguer time-reference of *another day* in sentence 6.) There is further reference to time within the incident itself: *an hour* (sentence 5) and *eventually* (sentence 8) which signals a connection of sequence with the sentences before it. The word *however* (sentence 4) also signals a connection, this time one of a logical alternative with the event in sentence 3.

There is a further element of cohesion which helps to create the discourse: the presence within it of words and phrases all of which belong within the general area of 'painting'. *Little gallery, picture, water colours, local artists, oil sketches, landscapes, interiors, finely-detailed study, lithograph, hand-coloured etching, Art Society* and *exhibition* – all belong within the same **semantic field** (general area of meaning). We can also learn a little of Laura's and her husband's taste in painting from reference to *landscape* (*rocks on the crest of a dark hillside* and *trees against a winter sunset*). Imagine the intrusion into this discourse of words and phrases in another, unrelated, semantic field (for instance, the word *rocket* for *rocks* and *missiles* for *trees*) and how, in such a case, the discourse would begin to stretch the reader's understanding of its meaning.

These words and phrases, then, connect the parts of the discourse together and so help to create a unified piece of language bigger than a single sentence. In part, we re-create the meaning of the discourse by embedding it within our knowledge of the world and making intelligent guesses as to its meaning. In subtle ways, the language refers *out from itself* to the world of the reader and in this way helps to make sense. Mostly, however, it is a result of the language referring *within itself* which builds up a coherent and complex meaning extending beyond its individual sentences.

Sound effects

Merely reading examples of discourse can give only a partial picture of how language communicates coherent sense. In written language, a **punctuation system** collaborates with the grammar to assist in the expression of meaning. The main sentence marks – full-stops, question marks and exclamation marks – are augmented by the comma, colon and semi-colon to *separate off* different words, phrases and clauses within each sentence, while the apostrophe and the inverted commas signal the *grammatical condition* of linguistic elements, the apostrophe *possession (John's house)* or *omission (Let's go out)* and inverted commas the fact that a stretch of language is spoken by someone other than the writer (or by the writer quoting him or herself). Without the punctuation system, it would be much harder to understand what we read, and sometimes impossible to sort out which of several possible meanings we should reconstruct from the written text. The same could be said for other conventions of the printed page: bold type, italics, capitals, underlinings and so on.

Spoken language, by contrast, has no punctuation. (This is one of the reasons why children find it difficult to learn to punctuate: there is no simple equivalent in speech on which they can build.) Instead, speech has a complex of systems of rhythms, pauses, stresses, melodies and tones – sound-effects which assist the grammar in communicating meaning. They can also express a great deal about the speaker's *attitude* to what is being said – something which, in writing, must be accomplished in different ways.

There are, for example, the **tones of voice** which allow us to say the same words in the same order but express quite different meanings. Consider, for example, how many ways there are of saying *Good morning!* expressing attitudes like pleasure, friendliness, boredom, even anger – all depending on the tone of voice adopted. These tones of voice are not usually a matter of personal preference in each speaker. If they were not understood by *all* speakers as part of a *shared* linguistic system, they could not communicate their meanings. Tones of voice, like certain facial expressions and body movements, are *systematic*: a part of the general linguistic behaviour of a speech community.

Other important systems are those of **stress** and **intonation**. Stress is the added loudness of volume placed on a spoken syllable to emphasise its importance within a larger linguistic element like a sentence. Contrast the different meanings expressed in these sentences, all of which share the same words in the same order:

> **I** don't want to go to Blackpool with the Jacksons!
> I **don't** want to go to Blackpool with the Jacksons!
> I don't **want** to go to Blackpool with the Jacksons!
> I don't want to **go** to Blackpool with the Jacksons!
> I don't want to go to **Black**pool with the Jacksons!
> I don't want to go to Blackpool with the **Jack**sons!

Intonation is the term given to the melody of spoken language – the behaviour of moving the **pitch** of the voice from its natural position up or down towards the extreme ranges of comfortable performance between the highest and lowest note a person can make in speech – the **pitch-range**.

For instance, there are many ways we can say *Yes* to the question:

> Do you like Indian food?

We could adopt a falling melody, beginning the word higher in the pitch-range than we finish it and gliding down as we say it. (Try this.) Depending on how high in the pitch-range we begin, and how far down we travel in the glide, we will express different attitudes, different degrees of 'yes-ness' in the reply. Try for yourself saying *yes* to express emphatic approval (starting very high and moving quite low); slightly less approval (starting lower and moving only a little way further down); and rather unenthusiastic assent (starting low and hardly moving down from there at all).

Then begin low down in the pitch-range and move upwards: first, to express cautious assent (starting low and not moving up very far); then as if you were going on to say something else (starting higher up and moving higher still). You may even like to try a more complex melody: starting fairly high, gliding down, and moving up again. (This should sound very doubtful indeed: as if you're about to go on to say: *but ...*).

Stress and intonation can also *work with the grammar* as one of a complex set of interrelated systems. Without them, we would have no way of superimposing upon the essential structure of a discourse our attitudes to what we are saying nor of emphasising those parts of the meaning which we want particularly to highlight. Indeed, there are occasions when, without stress and intonation, we would find it hard to make any sense at all. What, for instance, does this mean?

> He offered it to him but he decided to see whether she would like it instead. She looked at her and she indicated that she could accept it from him but not from him.

Any confusion we may feel in reading is cleared when we can *hear* the extra loudness on certain words or syllables caused by stress. In addition, the intonation will help in making the meaning clear. Try to read the same passage aloud, using the numbers below to make sure you know who is being referred to. Note the way your use of intonation and stress helps to clarify the meaning.

> He (1) offered it to him (2) but he (2) decided to see whether she (3) would like it instead. She (3) looked at her (4) and she (4) indicated that she (3) could accept it from him (2) but not from him (1).

Function and context

In fact, it is usually impossible to understand exactly what a piece of language means without knowing the **context** in which it is expressed. How helpful it would have been, in the last example, to have the people referred to in front of us so we could actually point to them as we spoke the words. Language is *used in the world* and interacts with its many contexts of use, changing its **forms** (its words, grammar, pronunciation, intonation, etc) to match its **functions**.

We have seen how sentence types (statements, commands, exclamations and questions) give *grammatical* indications of their function. For instance, commands leave out the SUBJECT of a statement sentence:

[You] Shut that door!

and yes/no-questions reverse the order of the SUBJECT and the auxiliary verb in the equivalent statement:

> He was coming on Monday.
> Was he coming on Monday?

These are instances of how grammar and function are closely related, the manipulation of grammar actually signalling the function of what is said – here, that the speaker is asking a question. (There would, of course, be intonation features here, too, to emphasise the questioning function.)

However, most of the functional possibilities of the language are brought about by less obvious means – and again context is usually essential in understanding how. For example, the request or order to close a door can be expressed in many ways:

> It's very cold in here, isn't it! Would you mind if I closed the door?

These two sentences suggest that the context is one in which the person speaking and the one addressed would probably not know each other very well. They are too polite for familiar contact and a possible reply might be:

> Yes it is. Let *me* do it!

The function, then, has been more than simply closing a door; it has involved being polite and cementing some kind of social connection. Contrast it with a more direct expression:

> It's freezing in here! Mind if we have the door shut?

where the tag question *isn't it?* becomes a direct statement; where *cold* is exaggerated to *freezing*; where the words *Do you* are elided; and where the SUBJECT of the subordinate clause in the second sentence changes from *I* to *we* – leaving it open as to who will close the door.

Even more direct is:

> It's freezing! Shut the door!

where all attempts at civility have gone as the sentences become a simple statement and a direct command.

> Were you born in a barn or something?

also suggests that the person addressed might close the door, but by now the explicit connection between the form of the language and its function is obscure indeed. Which introduces us to yet another set of descriptions: the ones which explain how we make **idioms** . . .

*   *   *

This book has tried to outline the basic grammatical systems of English and this chapter to show how, despite their power and influence, the making of language needs to use other systems too.

Within grammar alone, there is a great deal more to learn and, if you decide to continue into a deeper study, you will find yourself engrossed in a long and absorbing exploration. You will discover, for example, that grammarians talk a lot about different **models** of grammar – ways of describing how the language works from differing theoretical perspectives (and often using different meta-linguistic terms). You will find that they distinguish between grammars (like this one) which are **descriptive** and those which are **prescriptive**, instructing their readers in the rules of correct language use (and consequently often used by foreign language learners). They will also talk about **theoretical** grammars: ones which are not much concerned with describing in detail the vast linguistic sprawl of a language community but which seek instead to answer more fundamental questions, like *how* and *why* does all this come to happen? (Reading some of these grammatical descriptions is not unlike reading a book on algebra.) Above all, you will find that grammarians sometimes disagree.

They will, however, agree on this: that learning about grammar is to learn about a very deeply-rooted part of human behaviour. Grammar is, after all, inside the heads of human beings. Learning about the grammar of a language – like English – is to learn a great deal about the nature of English-speaking people and their language communities (since grammar is, as well, on the outside, in the society in which its speakers and writers exist).

But grammar, as we have seen, is only part of the process of making language. It assists us in expressing *meanings*. The study of meaning is called **semantics** . . .

But that is another book.

PART THREE

METALINGUISTIC TERMS

This section is for quick reference. The number in brackets refers to the page in the main text where the term is first dealt with in any detail. Words in small capitals refer to other items in this glossary.

accent (14)   The way a language is pronounced. People have different accents, often because of the region or social or ethnic group from which they come.

active voice (56)   To be contrasted with PASSIVE VOICE, an active SENTENCE is one in which the SUBJECT performs the action in the VERB (*Mark grasped the idea.*) The passive equivalent would be *The idea was grasped by Mark.*

adjective (31)   A class of WORD. Adjectives can occur before a NOUN (*the* **unpleasant** *smell*) or after certain VERBS (*The smell was* **fragrant**).

adjective phrase (39)   A WORD or group of words with an ADJECTIVE as the HEAD-WORD. Adjective phrases are commonly used as the SUBJECT COMPLEMENT in an SVC CLAUSE (*She looked* **very ill indeed**).

adverb (35)   A class of WORD. Adverbs are of many kinds. They can, for example, say more about the action in a VERB (*Jack fell* **gently**) or an ADJECTIVE (*I think you're* **absolutely** *terrific*) or indicate place (**There** *it is*). They can express the attitude of the speaker to what is said (**Regrettably,** *I shan't be there on Monday*). They can signal the connection between CLAUSES, either in terms of sequence (**Thirdly,** *he stole my wallet*) or logical relation (**However,** *he left the silver in the cupboard*).

ADVERBIAL (A) (60)   One of the elements of CLAUSE structure. In some cases (see SVA and SVOA structures) they are obligatory. In most clauses, however, they are optional elements (unlike the others). They are also the most mobile of the clause elements. Generally, they express more about the event in the clause (*He came* **on Saturday.** *Janet ran* **quickly**) or comment on the clause itself (**As a matter of fact,** *it wasn't too bad*). They can also link one clause to another in sequence (**Secondly,** *I should like to say . . .*) or logically (**Nonetheless,** *I think you'll agree . . .*). See ADVERB.

adverb phrase (39)   A WORD or group of words with an ADVERB as the HEAD-WORD (*very* **cheaply** *indeed*).

affix (26)   An INFLECTION; *words* can have their shapes changed by the addition of an affix (*call/call***ed**). See PREFIX and SUFFIX.

article (33)   The WORDS *a* (or *an*) and *the*. Articles help to specify the status of the NOUN they occur before, marking the contrast between, for example, *a car* and *the car* – the second being specified where the first is not.

aspect (47)   A property of the VERB PHRASE which expresses the duration of the action. In *She* **is weeping**, the action continues across time (contrast *She* **weeps**). Alternatively, aspect can express the fact that an action, starting in the past, is still continuing (*She* **has lived** *there for years*) as opposed to one in the past and now over (*She* **lived** *there for years*). See also TENSE.

auxiliary verb (46)   A verb occurring before a LEXICAL VERB in a VERB PHRASE (*She* **does** *love you. He* **is** *falling. You* **have** *finished.*) They can be used together in certain combinations (*Jenny* **has been** *trying*). Some auxiliary verbs may only be used before the lexical verb in verb phrases (*He* **must** *be there. You* **can't** *mean that. They* **shouldn't** *be long*). Others can also be used in their own right as lexical verbs (*I* **do.** *I* **am,** *but what I* **am** *none knows or cares. You* **have** *a very interesting tube of toothpaste*).

bound morpheme (26)   To be contrasted with a FREE MORPHEME, one which cannot stand on its own as a self-contained element. Such morphemes signal different grammatical FUNCTIONS, for instance the difference in number when the {plural} bound morpheme is added (*sword/sword***s**). See INFLECTION.

clause (50)   A unit of SENTENCE structure in which a VERB element holds other CLAUSE ELEMENTS in a structured relation both with itself and with each other. See also SUBORDINATE CLAUSE.

clause elements (50)   Each CLAUSE may contain a combination of linguistic elements (WORDS, PHRASES and/or other clauses) which serve particular functions within the total environment of the clause. These elements gain their identity as a result of the VERB element, the one essential in any clause. See SUBJECT, the OBJECTS, the COMPLEMENTS, the ADVERBIAL and the VERB element for details of each.

closed set (35)   When attributing the WORDS in the LEXICON to particular WORD-CLASSES, we see that some contain only small numbers of items and that it will be difficult to add new ones, these sets of words therefore being 'closed'. The closed sets are ARTICLES, DETERMINERS, PRONOUNS, PREPOSITIONS, CONJUNCTIONS and INTERJECTIONS. See also OPEN CLASSES.

cohesion (81)   The capacity of language to make connections across the boundaries of its PHRASES, CLAUSES and SENTENCES. Cohesion results from several interrelated systems: see, for example, REFERENCE. Without cohesion, DISCOURSE would not be possible.

command (66)   One of the four MAJOR SENTENCE types. Commands have a structure which distinguishes them from the other three types (STATEMENTS, EXCLAMATIONS and QUESTIONS). Some are made by ELLIPSIS of the SUBJECT ([you] *Do it*); some by using the VERB *let* (*Let's do it*).

common core (13)   In contrasting different DIALECTS of the same language, nonetheless the majority of its LEXICON, GRAMMAR and pronunciation will be shared. This is the common core of the language.

complex sentence (63)   A sentence which consists of more than one CLAUSE and in which at least one has been SUBORDINATED as one of its constituent elements. In *When I get home, I'll have supper*, the ADVERBIAL *When I get home* is itself a CLAUSE with a SUBJECT *I*, a VERB *get* and an ADVERBIAL *home*, the clause being connected to the SUPERORDINATE CLAUSE by the SUBORDINATING CONJUNCTION *when*. Compare with COMPOUND SENTENCES.

compound sentence (63)   A SENTENCE in which two or more CLAUSES are joined in equal balance within the whole sentence by a

CO-ORDINATING CONJUNCTION (*I like butter* **but** *I don't like syrup*). Contrast compound sentences with COMPLEX SENTENCES in which clauses are joined in unequal balance, with one or more being subordinated as a component in the whole structure.

concord (45)   Grammatical behaviour in which WORDS must agree with one another. The present tense VERB PHRASE must be INFLECTED if its SUBJECT is 3rd person singular (*I sing, He sings*).

conjunction (70)   A WORD used to join together two other linguistic elements. Conjunctions at PHRASE LEVEL can join words inside the same phrase (*cold* **but** *happy; singing* **and** *dancing*). At CLAUSE level they can join clauses (*I saw Tom* **but** *he didn't see me. It was warm* **although** *the wind was blowing*).

context (86)   The conditions in which a linguistic utterance is made. Context will involve the nature of the speaker/writer; his/her relationship with the listener or reader; the circumstance in which the utterance is made (eg: time, place, etc.); the topic; and other variables.

co-ordinating conjunction (70)   (also **co-ordinator**) A WORD used to co-ordinate two words, PHRASES or CLAUSES into a compound unit (*wine* **or** *beer; the woman in black* **and** *the girl in green; She was poor* **but** *she was honest*).

determiner (35, 42)   A WORD which determines the status of the NOUN in a NOUN PHRASE. It may be used in place of, but not as well as, the ARTICLE and will determine, for example, whether the noun is singular or plural (**This** *hat*/**These** *hats*), who it belongs to (**My** *hat*/**Your** *hat*), whether it is countable or mass (**Some** *puddings*/**Any** *pudding*) etc.

dialect (13)   A major variety of any language, normally associated with region and sometimes with class. Dialects are identified by features of the LEXICON and the GRAMMAR. Usually, they are also associated with sound features (ACCENT) but this is not a necessary condition of dialect since it is possible to speak dialect 'A' with accent 'B' and the written form of a language will also be in one of its dialects. See also STANDARD ENGLISH DIALECT.

DIRECT OBJECT (O) (55)   One of the CLAUSE ELEMENTS resulting in SVO, SVOO and SVOA clauses. The DIRECT OBJECT results from the use of a TRANSITIVE VERB enabling an EXTENSIVE relationship to exist between SUBJECT and OBJECT (*Nora bashed* **the doctor**).

discourse (79)   Any self-contained stretch of language. It is occasionally possible to find one consisting of only a single SENTENCE. However, this is rare and so discourse is normally taken to mean any stretch of language longer than a single sentence.

dummy subject (53)   In order to construct a complete CLAUSE, it is sometimes necessary to use a SUBJECT which has no meaning but which fulfils the structural requirement for a SUBJECT in the CLAUSE (**It**'*s raining.* **There**'*s trouble at the mill*).

ellipsis (76)   We often omit linguistic elements which have already occurred in the words recently uttered. This is ellipsis. (Q: *Where are you going?* A: **To the zoo.** – where *I am going* has been **elided**).

exclamation (67)   One of the four MAJOR SENTENCE types. Exclamations have a structure which distinguishes them from the other three types (see STATEMENTS, COMMANDS and QUESTIONS). They begin with a 'WH'-word (**What** *an astonishing idea!* **How** *remarkable it was!*) and, in the latter case, show a structural closeness to an equivalent QUESTION: *How remarkable was it?*

extensive verb (54)   A VERB which does not allow a close SEMANTIC relationship between its SUBJECT and the CLAUSE ELEMENT following (*Clare* **licked** *the icecream*). Contrast with INTENSIVE VERB.

finite (75)   The state of the VERB in a CLAUSE is either finite or NON-FINITE. Where finite, it may stand on its own as the MAIN VERB in the structure (*John* **can see**). Contrast this with the unacceptable clause which would result from a non-finite verb being used (*John having seen. John to see*). However, such clauses become acceptable when used as SUBORDINATE CLAUSES (*John,* **having seen** *him, decided to employ him.*)

free morpheme (26)   Where a MORPHEME may stand on its own as a free-standing linguistic element, it is 'free' as opposed to 'bound'. Many WORDS consist of free morphemes (*dog, cat, beauty, truth*), some of combinations of free morphemes (*keyboard, hillside*) while others are combinations of free and BOUND morphemes (*sing-ing, freckle-s, sad-ness*).

function Two meanings can be applied to this term. Firstly (19, 86) the uses to which language-users put language (eg: description, warning, humour, seduction, explanation, etc). Secondly (34) in the context of language structure, how a linguistic element functions within a given structure. For instance, *the car* functions as SUBJECT in *The car had broken down* but as DIRECT OBJECT in *Sam couldn't start the car*.

future (46) Often referred to as 'future tense', future is a time relation. There are several ways of expressing futurity in our language. Certain AUXILIARY VERBS imply that the event in the VERB has not yet taken place (*I **will** be there; You **must** stop doing that; I'm **going to** arrive*). Another way is with a time ADVERBIAL (*I'm coming **tomorrow***). Notice the importance of the combination of verb form and ADVERBIAL to express futurity. (See TENSE.)

grammar (19) The elements of language structure; their internal behaviour; the rules which organise how they may or may not be combined together; and their behaviour when in the presence of other elements. All languages have a grammar. This is generally understood to embrace its MORPHOLOGY (the MORPHEMES and the rules for combining them) and its SYNTAX, which deals with units of structure larger than morphemes (and in particular the nature of SENTENCES). 'Grammar' also means the study of such linguistic behaviour.

head-word (39) The WORD which establishes the identity of a PHRASE in that any other words in that phrase must relate to the head-word. An ADJECTIVE PHRASE, for example, will have an ADJECTIVE as its head-word, while a VERB PHRASE will be so because it has a VERB as its head-word.

idiolect (18) The unique variety of speaking/writing of an individual language-user. Everyone has his or her own idiolect.

INDIRECT OBJECT (Oi) (58) One of the CLAUSE ELEMENTS. An INDIRECT OBJECT is found when a clause already contains a DIRECT OBJECT. In terms of its meaning, it fulfils a recipient role (*I gave* **Alan** *the news*).

inflection (28) When the shape of a WORD is changed in order to mark some grammatical contrast; for instance, that between singular and plural (*cup, cups*), or between first and third person singular present tense (*make, makes*) or between present and past (*call, called*).

intensive verb (54)   A VERB is intensive if it allows a relationship to hold between the SUBJECT of the CLAUSE and the CLAUSE ELEMENT following, in which there is a strong SEMANTIC connection between the two, as in SVC structures (*Jonathan* **was** *a historian*).

interjection (35)   A class of WORD. Interjections express surprise (*Gosh!*), pain (*Ouch!*), simple response (*Oh!*), etc.

intonation (85)   One of a system of sound effects; the 'melodies' of spoken language, in which the voice PITCH systematically moves up and down within the pitch-range to express attitude and to emphasise meaning.

intransitive verb (55)   A VERB is intransitive if it does not effect the relationship between the SUBJECT of the CLAUSE and an OBJECT (*The dogs* **bark**). However, most VERBs can be used either intransitively (*Mark* **is reading**) or transitively (*Mark* **is reading** *sociology books*). See also SV structures and TRANSITIVE VERB.

level   The term has two major meanings: (20) language is said to exist simultaneously at the three levels of sound, meaning and structure (the **phonological, semantic** and **grammatical** levels); (21) in GRAMMAR, levels also exist, the lowest being that of the MORPHEME. Succeeding levels are WORD, PHRASE, CLAUSE and the highest level of all, SENTENCE. Thus language structure can be seen to be hierarchical.

lexical verb (44)   In a VERB PHRASE, the lexical verb is the HEADWORD, carrying the main meaning (**Run,** *am going to* **fall,** *used to be trying to* **win**). The lexical verb comes last in the phrase. Contrast with AUXILIARY VERB.

lexicon (31)   The word stock of a language, commonly known as the 'vocabulary'.

linguistics (8)   The scientific study of human language.

main verb (76)   In COMPLEX SENTENCES we distinguish between the VERB in the SUPERORDINATE CLAUSE and those in any SUB-

ORDINATE CLAUSES by calling it the main verb. In the SENTENCE *Sue watched the seagull when it landed on the beach*, the main verb is *watched*.

major sentence (65)   To distinguish between SENTENCES which are essentially ready-made and all the rest, we split them into two classes: major and MINOR. Major sentences are made as a result of PRODUCTIVE rules of grammar which allow the creation of an infinite number of different major sentence structures.

metalanguage (7)   The language used about language itself. This glossary contains a list of **metalinguistic** terms.

minor sentence (65)   Unlike MAJOR SENTENCES, which result from the PRODUCTIVE rules of grammar, minor sentences are, on the whole, unproductive (though occasionally with some space for the user to fill in prescribed gaps, as in *Long live . . . X* and *Down with . . . Y*). Minor sentences are used a lot in conversation for responses (*Yes. No. Sorry*), in greeting and parting (*Hello. Goodbye. Cheerio*) and in written notices (*Exit*). See MAJOR SENTENCES.

morpheme (25)   The lowest element of GRAMMAR. See BOUND and FREE MORPHEME.

morphology (29)   One of the two essential dimensions of GRAMMAR (the other being SYNTAX). Morphology is concerned with the formation of WORDS and the structural properties and behaviour of MORPHEMES.

non-finite (75)   The state of a VERB in a CLAUSE is either FINITE or non-finite. When it is in its non-finite state, it cannot stand as the MAIN VERB in the clause (*Sheila* **to win** *the race. Angela* **losing** *the money*). However, non-finite verbs can be used in SUBORDINATE CLAUSES (*Angela* **losing** *the race was disappointing. For Sheila* **to win** *the race was what we all wanted most*). A subordinate clause made in this way is called a **non-finite clause**.

noun (35)   A class of WORD. A noun may function, for example, as the SUBJECT of a SENTENCE (**Albert** *spat*) and may be INFLECTED for plural (*Cat/Cats*).

noun phrase (39)   A PHRASE with a NOUN or a PRONOUN as its HEAD-WORD (*One of those things, my sister, unhappiness, him*).

OBJECT COMPLEMENT (Co) (59)   A CLAUSE ELEMENT which fulfils a comparable function to the COMPLEMENT in SVC structures, but this time relating directly to the OBJECT. *The judge declared the question* **out of order** can be analysed as: *The judge* (SUBJECT) *declared* (VERB) *the question* (OBJECT) **out of order** (OBJECT COMPLEMENT).

open class (35)   When attributing WORDS in the LEXICON to particular WORD-CLASSES, we see that some belong to very large classes which are being enlarged by the constant addition of new items. These classes are, therefore, open. The open classes are NOUNS, VERBS, ADJECTIVES and ADVERBS. Contrast with CLOSED SETS.

passive voice (56)   A TRANSITIVE VERB may be used in an ACTIVE mode (*Tom* **ate** *fish*) or in its passive equivalent (*Fish* **was eaten** *by Tom*). In the second example, the SUBJECT of the active SENTENCE has been moved to the agent position (with the addition of the PREPOSITION *by*), the verb has been INFLECTED with *-en*, the AUXILIARY VERB *was* has been added and the original DIRECT OBJECT has become the SUBJECT of the new, passive, structure.

phrasal verb (44)   A VERB which includes a 'particle' as well as a LEXICAL VERB (*sum* **up**, *cave* **in**, *make* **up for**).

phrase (37)   One of the LEVELS of GRAMMAR. A phrase may consist of one or more WORDS (*honey/that absolutely delicious honey*) and all but one kind will centre upon a HEAD-WORD. (The exception is the PREPOSITIONAL PHRASE.) See also NOUN PHRASE, VERB PHRASE, ADJECTIVE PHRASE and ADVERB PHRASE.

pitch (85)   Part of the sound system of a language; the movement of the spoken voice between the highest and lowest parts of the **pitch-range**. See INTONATION.

prefix (26)   An INFLECTION which occurs on the beginning of a WORD (**un***happy*). See also AFFIX and SUFFIX.

preposition (35)   A class of WORD. Generally, prepositions serve a joining function, connecting NOUN or ADVERB PHRASES to other elements (*the old wooden seat* **in** *the garden* **under** *the tree* **by** *the flowerbed* **over** *there*) and come before those elements (hence the name).

prepositional phrase (39)   One of the PHRASE groups in English. Such phrases consist of a PREPOSITION followed by other words to create a single phrase (**in** *the corner;* **at** *best;* **under** *here*).

productivity (19, 64)   The capacity of grammar to generate a limitless number of structures from a finite number of elements. See MAJOR SENTENCE.

pronoun (35)   A class of WORD. Pronouns may take the place of NOUN PHRASES as the SUBJECT of a SENTENCE (*My friend Pete's been hurt.* **He** *fell off that roof*). They are INFLECTED to indicate their FUNCTION within the CLAUSE (**He** *wanted a pencil. I gave it to* **him.** *He returned it to* **me**) or to express possession (*Pete's pencil was blunt.* **Mine** was sharp). See also RELATIVE PRONOUN.

question (67)   One of the four MAJOR SENTENCE types. Questions have structural features which distinguish them from the other three types (see STATEMENTS, EXCLAMATIONS and COMMANDS). Questions fall into several different categories depending partly on structure and partly on intention: 'yes/no' (*Has my brother been here today?*); 'WH' (*When did you last see him?*); 'either/or' (*Did he come here or go straight to the airport?*) and 'tag' (*He's been here already, hasn't he?*).

Received Pronunciation ('RP') (16)   The technical label for the ACCENT of British English most often heard among educated middle-class speakers and on the broadcast media (hence its popular label: 'BBC English'). It is an accent impossible to distinguish on a regional basis.

reference (81)   One of the systems of COHESION in which **reference items** refer across boundaries to other linguistic items (*The man sat in the pub.* **He** *was alone* **there**) or to **referents** in the non-linguistic world (*Look at* **that**).

register (17)   A variety of language, sometimes specific to professional groups (eg: doctors). We adopt different registers depending on the CONTEXT in which we use language (contrast STYLES of journalism in newspapers aimed at different kinds of reader).

relative clause (73)   A CLAUSE which relates to the HEAD-WORD of a NOUN PHRASE (. . . *that bicycle* **which you stole from William**). It is introduced with a RELATIVE PRONOUN (*which* in this example) though this may be omitted through ELLIPSIS (*the priest* [whom] **we found in the jungle**). Unlike other forms of SUBORDINATE CLAUSE, a relative clause forms only part, and not the whole, of a constituent CLAUSE ELEMENT in the SUPERORDINATE clause.

relative pronoun (74)   A PRONOUN which enables the construction of a RELATIVE CLAUSE (*the things* **that** *I enjoy most*).

semantic field (83)   The collection of words and phrases which are associated with a particular area of meaning. (For example, the words *football*, *tennis court* and *hockey stick* all belong within the semantic field 'sport'.)

semantics (88)   The study of linguistic meaning. The semantic LEVEL is one of the three LEVELS of language.

sentence (22)   The highest grammatical element (see LEVELS). For more detail, see MAJOR and MINOR SENTENCES.

simple sentence (63)   A sentence containing only one CLAUSE. Contrast with COMPLEX and COMPOUND SENTENCES.

Standard English Dialect ('SE') (16)   The DIALECT of English spoken by the majority of educated, middle-class speakers, most often heard in the media and used in most written language.

statement (66)   One of the four MAJOR SENTENCE types and the most common. Broadly speaking, statements give information. They have a variety of structural features. Typically, they begin with a SUBJECT, then a VERB and then other, related, elements (*She went to town*). Such structures distinguish statements from other sentence types. See COMMANDS, EXCLAMATIONS and QUESTIONS.

stress (85)   One of the sound systems of a language; the increasing of loudness on a syllable. Stress helps to express attitude and to emphasise meaning.

style (17)   Particular ways of speaking or writing in which the language-user matches the form of expression to its CONTEXT. Style may be described in terms of certain formal features (eg: GRAMMAR, vocabulary and features of pronunciation, etc).

SUBJECT (S) (52)   One of the CLAUSE ELEMENTS. The SUBJECT, alone among clause elements, must agree with the VERB (**You** *agree*/**She** *agrees*; see CONCORD). Its favourite position in the CLAUSE is at the beginning (**The hiker** *came slowly down the hill*) but this is not an absolute rule (*Slowly down the hill came* **the hiker**). Normally, the SUBJECT performs the action in the VERB, but not in PASSIVE sentences (**She** *ate the sandwich.* **The sandwich** *was eaten by her*).

SUBJECT COMPLEMENT (C) (57) One of the CLAUSE ELEMENTS. The SUBJECT COMPLEMENT is related to the SUBJECT by an INTENSIVE VERB. It refers to the same thing or person as the SUBJECT itself (*She is* **my wife**. *The dentist feels* **groggy**).

subordinate clause (71) In a COMPLEX SENTENCE, one or more CLAUSES may be joined to it as constituent elements. Thus, the SUBJECT in the sentence **That he was angry** *appeared obvious* itself contains elements of clause structure: *He* (SUBJECT) *was* (VERB) *angry* (COMPLEMENT). Subordinate clauses are hierarchically at a lower LEVEL than their SUPERORDINATE CLAUSE because they constitute part of that higher-level structure. Subordinate clauses may be put one inside the other ([**Because the train was late [when we arrived at the station]**] *we didn't get here until midnight*).

subordinating conjunction (71) (also **subordinator**) A WORD used to connect a SUBORDINATE CLAUSE to a CLAUSE at a higher LEVEL (*I like you* **because** *you're good at tennis*).

suffix (26) An INFLECTION which occurs on the end of a WORD (*happen***ing**). See also AFFIX and PREFIX.

superordinate clause (75) In COMPLEX SENTENCES, in which one or more SUBORDINATE CLAUSES occur, the CLAUSE of which they are constituent elements, and which therefore operates higher in LEVEL, is called the superordinate clause. In the sentence *Before I could get my bearings, the lights went out* the subordinate clause is *Before I could get my bearings*. This clause functions as the ADVERBIAL in the clause at the level above (in this case, the whole sentence). Hence this higher-level clause is superordinate. See also SUB-ORDINATE CLAUSE.

SV (55) A type of CLAUSE consisting of a SUBJECT and a VERB (*The dogs barked*).

SVA (61)   A type of CLAUSE consisting of a SUBJECT, VERB and an ADVERBIAL (*Clare was in the garden*).

SVC (57)   A type of CLAUSE consisting of a SUBJECT, VERB and SUBJECT COMPLEMENT (*Susan is a nurse. Tony seems unhappy*).

SVO (56)   A type of CLAUSE consisting of a SUBJECT, VERB and DIRECT OBJECT (*My boss has lost her marbles*).

SVOA (61)   A type of CLAUSE consisting of a SUBJECT, VERB, DIRECT OBJECT and an ADVERBIAL (*The surgeon placed the matron on the operating table*).

SVOC (59)   A type of CLAUSE consisting of a SUBJECT, VERB, DIRECT OBJECT and OBJECT COMPLEMENT (*That book made him thoughtful*).

SVOO (58)   A type of CLAUSE consisting of a SUBJECT, VERB, DIRECT and INDIRECT OBJECT (*They offered the butler the rope*).

syntax (29)   One of the two essential dimensions of GRAMMAR (the other being MORPHOLOGY). Syntax embraces the behaviour and relationships of elements bigger than morphemes. Hence its concern is with the structural properties of WORDS, PHRASES, CLAUSES and SENTENCES.

tense (46)   A VERB may be INFLECTED to signal a change in tense. There are two tenses in English: past and present. See also FUTURE.

transitive verb (55)   A VERB which effects a relationship between the SUBJECT and an OBJECT (*Jonathan **recited** his first poem*). Contrast with a verb used INTRANSITIVELY where this does not happen (*Jonathan **recited***).

verb (35)   A class of WORD. Verbs express actions (*hit*) and states of being (*am*). See also AUXILIARY VERB, LEXICAL VERB and VERB PHRASE.

VERB (50)   The crucial element in the CLAUSE for, without this, the clause could not exist. It effects the relationship between all other CLAUSE ELEMENTS and endows them with their identity. For example, the PHRASE *the cat* functions as the SUBJECT of the first, and the DIRECT OBJECT of the second example following because of its position relative to the VERB element: *The cat* **spat** *in the dog's face. The dog* **bit** *the cat.*

verb phrase (39)   A PHRASE with a VERB as its HEAD-WORD. See also AUXILIARY VERB, LEXICAL VERB and VERB.

verbless clause (78)   A CLAUSE without a VERB (**Happy with his winnings,** *Pete went out and bought a new car*). We can reconstruct a full clause on the basis of certain elements having been omitted through ELLIPSIS ([He was] *happy with his winnings . . .*).

word (31)   An item in the LEXICON. Structurally, words stand between MORPHEMES and PHRASES in the hierarchy of structural LEVELS.

word-class (31)   Traditionally known as **parts-of-speech**, a set of categories to which the WORDS in the LEXICON may be allocated on the basis of their grammatical FUNCTION in the CLAUSE. Hence the word *singing* may belong to the class of ADJECTIVES (*There's a* **singing** *noise in my ears*), NOUNS (*Tom hates* **singing**) or VERBS (*She'll be* **singing** *in the bath all night*) depending on its use in the clause. Words belong within four OPEN CLASSES and six CLOSED SETS (see page 35).